OFFICE ACCESS

Y0-CBW-917

2	**INTRODUCTION**
8	**THE PEOPLE**
18	PERFORMANCE
20	POWER
24	PROXIMITY
32	**THE TOOLS**
32	STORAGE
40	SURFACES
46	SEATING
50	**THE PLACE**
55	SIGHT
60	LIGHT
64	SOUND
66	**THE OFFICE**
69	THEN
72	NOW
77	NEXT
82	**INVENTORY**
88	**BIBLIOGRAPHY**
92	**GLOSSARY**

INTROD

The purpose of this book is to empower you to ask the best questions of yourself and of the designers and architects who serve you in order to make your office perform better.

This book allows you to ask these questions whether you have six desks in a storefront travel agency or six hundred desks on the sixtieth floor of a sixty-story office building. The questions and the palette of available answers are the same.

We all need a place to work. But many of us do not know how to articulate our desire for the quality of where we work. This book will give you the vocabulary to express what a quality workplace means to you.

Many of us need to know the possibilities and availabilities that can influence the quality of the spaces in which we work. After all, we spend more time at work than in any other single space in our lives besides, perhaps, our beds.

Usually we think of the objects that fill our work spaces more than we think of the spaces between them, much as we focus on the buildings in a city more than the performance of the spaces between them. However, the quality of our cities has more to do with the spaces between buildings than with the

CTION

buildings themselves. The buildings of Venice are beautiful, but the quality of Venice's Piazza San Marco consists of more than the rather anonymous three-sided colonnade around it.

The experiences we have are in the spaces between things. That's where we do our living: the spaces between buildings, between walls or furniture, and between people. It's the organization of those spaces that allows not only better function, but artful function, which is **performance**. This is true of our work spaces as well as our living spaces.

There are **three major areas of concern** that relate to the design of an office. One has to do with the **organization** of the pieces in the office. In a small scale, these are the things on your desk; at a middle scale, it would be the desk's files and partitions in relation to each other; and at the most important scale, the **macro scale,** it's the groups of desks, workstations, and offices relative to other offices. At all scales the topics of **performance, power,** and **proximity** play an important role (we call these the three *P* words).

The second area of concern is the **physical objects** themselves, the physical possibilities of the office. Surfaces can be the floor, the wall, or the most common surface—the top of a

4

desk or table. The function of surfaces is in how they organize and present "space" for you to fill with useful activity. You can also have places to sit and places for storage, whether they are bookshelves, filing cabinets, or a computer. And these three things encompass what we call the three *S* words: **surfaces, seating,** and **storage.**

The third area has to do with `environmental concerns` that affect both the objects in and the organization of your office. These concerns have to do with **sight** (what and who you can see), **light** (the quality of artificial and natural light), and **sound** (what kinds of sound or lack of sound are useful and the benefits of overhearing.) Privacy and confidentiality. **Sight, light, and sound.**

`Emerging technologies` are a natural complement to this outline of basic concerns. Not only the telephone and the typewriter, but now the computer and the fax machine: how these machines affect where we need to be in order to do our work; where we need to be to work with others; how they are housed, located and changed; and how they influence the very nature of work itself.

But let's get back to the first point, which is the most important issue: how we organize an office, how we make decisions, how we think about ourselves for human interaction. The classic way of organizing an office looks much like the organizational chart of a company, with the chairman of the board and the president on top, and the rest of the organization moving down through a kind of pyramid-like structure. The person highest up on this `pyramid` has a relationship with the people next highest up on the pyramid, and so forth down the line. These relationships, however, are not necessarily the best relationships. Nor does this always represent the best way to maximize the appropriate interactions and performance of a company.

Lately, a number of management consultants have been saying we should turn the pyramid upside down, as a kind of radical alternative that exposes the relationship of company personnel to the public.

One immediately recognizable example of this "public contact" management is Disney World. We can't be expected to understand the complicated network of electronics, architecture, and facilities that operate there; all we see are marvelous attractions and a relentlessly efficient and smiling work force. Mickey Mouse *is* Disney World, as far as we know.

Another example of this `"reverse logic"` is McDonald's. Your dominant image of the incredibly successful fast-food establishment is derived from the interactions that take place when you order and pay for a Big Mac and fries.

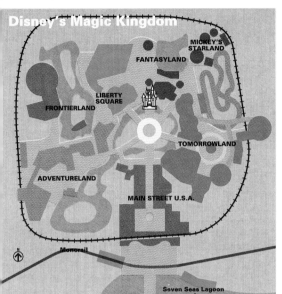

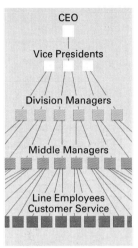

Line Employees
Customer Service

**Inverted
Pyramid
Organization**

CEO
CEO

**Traditional
Pyramid
Organization**

Line Employees
Customer Service

One way of organizing a corporation is through some hierarchical relationship—a pyramid on its base or point. A second way is to put the people who must work together next to each other. The clearest example is that of your secretary sitting next to you if you're an executive. Or if you're a secretary, your executive next to you. The people who have the most interaction are next to each other. This, of course, quite clearly promotes efficient visual contact.

One would say, "Well, why should we do it any other way?" This seems to be the best idea. However, such efficiency excludes the possibility of a certain level of serendipitous interaction among others not immediately or essentially involved in the relationship.

Henry Ford is credited with the organization and invention of the **assembly line,** in which workers had the narrowest knowledge of the total product. Each person did a simple, repetitive task, each adding incrementally to the making of an automobile.

What eventually occurred was the distancing of the worker from the knowledge of the total product. That person was also distanced from feeling ownership of that product, an image that was picked up wonderfully both by Charlie Chaplin in *Modern Times*, and in a hilarious sequence (if you can remember back that far) in *I Love Lucy*, when Lucy was dipping cherries into melted chocolate.

One of the most damaging aspects of this "efficiency" was the removal of responsibility for quality from those who were the most logical choice—the line workers who have the most impact on the product. If knowledge is kept from them, how can they be held accountable?

Volvo developed a way of organizing factories in which a team of people did multiple tasks instead of single tasks. And now the SATURN division of General Motors has a team of people virtually putting together a whole car, and essentially owning that car; you, the buyer, feel a team of people really stands behind the car you bought.

In order to gain the knowledge of the whole, you need to have a sense of other people and what they do, and you need to develop this sense in a relaxed, interested way, rather than in a flurry of concern over an immediate need. This is the essence of the worked-over notion of "team-building." People will work hard, but not be motivated, under relentless pressure. Sustaining motivation requires the patience that is essential to fostering work relationships strong enough to respond to high demand.

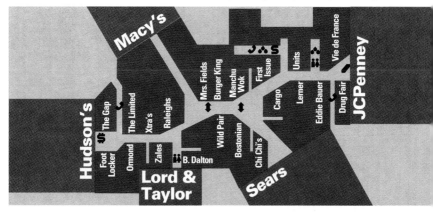

One layout that allows you to go about your business in a relaxed but well-organized way is the model of a shopping mall. If you substituted the offices of the president and the vice president at the opposite ends of an office floor plan for the department-store anchors in a mall, you would develop a positive tension between those offices/anchors. These destinations encourage shoppers to walk between them, and the walkway becomes a sort of information street. The walkway is what actually creates the mall/office. And it encourages pedestrian traffic that allows the shop owners/employees between the "anchors" to see and understand better what's going on.

The whole concept of the shopping mall is based on this stroll. You see things you wouldn't otherwise go to see and buy things you might not have bought. There are serendipitous meetings. Likewise, in an office, the traffic between the two anchors (president and vice president, CEO and CFO) creates the possibility for people to meet at the water fountain or the coffee machine, to pass by each other and gain a sense of what one another is doing through casual conversation—saying hello or looking at somebody's desk.

In the offices of The *Understanding*Business in San Francisco, the senior managers have their offices at the back of the office, on purpose. When visitors come to see the president, they have to walk through the whole office, so they get a sense of what goes on without being taken on a tour. In regular trips to get a cup of coffee or ride the elevator to the lobby, the office managers pass by people and think of things to say, or it occurs to them to ask about something, which keeps them involved in what's going on in the office. It was not a casual decision to place those offices where they are.

The **three organizational issues** we are discussing are **power,** which is the organizational pyramid; **proximity,** your secretary being next to you; and a kind of overall look at the ways of encouraging the **performance** of your office: what is your end goal? Is your end goal maximum privacy? Is it the exclusivity of power? Is it to have people know each other? How do you design the space between people and offices to encourage or discourage the kind of action/reaction and interaction that's desirable?

If your scale is a small agency or office, what is the public realm? And the realm of the worker? How important is privacy, and how important is it for a travel agent to turn to one of his or her fellow workers and say, "I haven't been to Belize, have you? Can you help me?" How important is it to overhear what somebody says so you can offer that kind of suggestive response and useful service, or is it better for you to have the utmost privacy so nobody hears anything you are saying? In a job interview or a medical discussion you have one end of the scale of privacy. And on the other end of the scale, in an R&D environment, for example, you want to have as much help as you can from as many people as there are to pool resources for optimum performance. That's the continuum that you want to think about.

The purpose of this book is to **empower** you—empower you to get the kind of answers, the kind of suggestions, and the kind of design that will improve the quality of the time you spend at work. Parenthetically, you might want to go home and rearrange your living room.

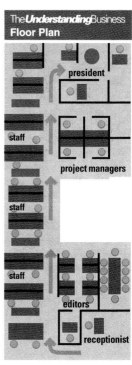

The *Understanding*Business
Floor Plan

president

staff

project managers

staff

staff

editors

receptionist

THE PE

THE PEOPLE

The three topics and sections in this chapter are:

Performance

Power

Proximity

office workers consider effect of environment on productivity

69%	Very Important
28%	Somewhat Important
2%	Not Very Important
1%	Not At All Important
0%	Not Sure

office workers assess current environment

23%	Excellent
50%	Good
21%	Only Fair
6%	Poor

Source: 1989 Worldwide Office Environment Index (OEI), conducted by Louis Harris & Assoc.

THE DYNAMICS OF DESIGN

Design is about information, instructions, and ideas. In exploring design, this book is a lot about **what** an office is and somewhat about **how** an office can be most effective. This book raises questions and encourages people who own, manage, and work in offices to look at all the options available to them in designing their work environment.

This is a "what if" book more than it is a "how to" book.

Before designing your own office, take a look at the myths surrounding office design and behavior. Some of the myths are vintage, some are recent developments. Some need to be rethought, while others should be tossed out entirely.

The perceived need for well-designed, pleasant, functional office space really has taken root in the past 10 to 15 years. While we can safely assume that people will continue to work for the foreseeable future, we can no longer abide by previous assumptions about who works, why they work, where they work, and how they work. If business is in a flux (and when isn't it?), it's a safe bet to assume the office enclosing a business and the thinking behind that office are likewise in constant motion.

PLE

office workers are working at top productivity	
48%	1991
49%	1989
47%	1988
46%	1986
42%	1978
Office workers who agree	
33%	1991
21%	1989
24%	1988
16%	1986
NA	1978
Top executives who agree	

OEI Survey 1991

This book will give you **clues** to successful office design. The three largest sections are about the **people** in an office, the **tools** they use, and the **space** that surrounds them. The constant, obviously, is people. And since any effective design has a measure of anticipation and preparedness, this book includes a section about **trends** in technology and work habits, as well.

People at Work

The image most people have of an office, which has shaped most thinking about offices, is something along the lines of the insurance company where Jack Lemmon and Shirley MacLaine worked in the movie *The Apartment,* circa 1960. It doesn't matter that many people have never seen this 30-year-old classic—its images of men in suits, women in uncomfortable shoes, rows upon rows of desks (populated by employees who have no idea of the larger operations of "the business"), high-speed elevators, and even scheming politics form the collective mental picture most people summon up when they think of an office.

And yet, since the mid '80s, less than 50% of the North American workforce has been made up of white males; a glance through the commercial real estate listings of any large city

Work consists of whatever a body is obliged to do, and play consists of whatever a body is not obliged to do.

Mark Twain

Work expands so as to fill the time available for its completion [and] the thing to be done swells in importance and complexity in a direct ratio with the time to be spent.

C. Northcote Parkinson

Office/Company Organizations

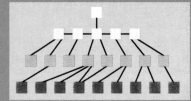

Hierarchical

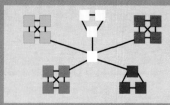

Teams or Quality Circles

newspaper confirms the trend away from high-rise buildings housing thousands of daytime commuters; a trip by automobile around New York, Chicago, Los Angeles, or Toronto quickly evaporates the notion of **"rush hour"** (there's "slow hour" and "slower hour") and that's because people work on different schedules than they used to and they work all over the place. This is more than **"reverse commuting,"** it's **"diverse commuting."** Perhaps the most significant change of all is one that a walk through the office shows you: where are all the metal desks and chairs, the noisy typewriters, the carbon paper, the switchboards, the rotary dial phones?

As is often the case, the practical behavior that is the essence of business has evolved more rapidly than the "expert" thinking and physical environments that explain and support it. The complicated, multiperson and multitalent demands of our present **Information Society** are still routinely performed in the one-person/one-desk/one-task offices of a different era.

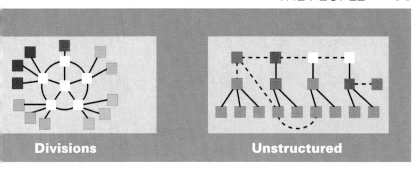

Divisions   **Unstructured**

"Well, Baxter, you got your promotion. Sometime when it's feasible I'd like to shake your hand."

Harvard Business Review

...a thick glass door protects the entrance to The Fourteenth Floor. It is electronically locked and is opened by a receptionist who actuates a switch under her desk in a large, plain waiting room outside the door.

Once inside, the eerie silence reinforced an impression of great power.

...The atmosphere on the Fourteenth Floor is awesomely quiet. The hallways are usually deserted. People speak in hushed voices. The omnipresent quiet projects an aura of awesome power. The reason it is so quiet must mean that General Motors' powerful executives are hard at work in their offices studying problems, analyzing mountains of complicated data, holding meetings and making important, calculated business decisions. There is no room for laughter or casual conversations in the halls. There is too much work to be done to be frivolous.

J. Patrick Wright with John Z. DeLorean, *On a Clear Day You Can See General Motors*

thing the Point:
formance, Power, and Proximity

MYTH 1: One's title and place on the corporate organiza- chart should determine the location, size, and furnishings ne's office.

For the past 100 years, it hasn't mattered that the division head and the people you deal with on a daily basis are six rs removed, or that the Vice President of Sales may have a y different job than the Vice President of Finance—both re- ed a big wooden desk, a leather chair, a credenza, a secre- outside the door, and a Bigelow carpet on the floor.

Whether this hierarchical structure was ever appropriate, whether it was simply the imposition of a military-style ad- istration on a civilian workforce, is a matter for conjecture. present reality, however, is one of multiple layers of **ponsibility** within every level of an organization, which rly runs counter to the separatism of the classic hierarchy. a short-sighted salesperson who doesn't understand his pany's accounting system. An automobile designer had er be listening to marketing people, who, in turn, should be ng to customers. The human resources director who isn't nately acquainted with the company's products and ser- s will be a dismal failure. And, of course, a rigid hierarchi- structure never works well in a small business anyway. ardless of the size of his or her desk, the owner of a small ness is still chief executive officer and receptionist.

perceived hazards in the office workspace

charts indicate percentage who consider item "very" or "somewhat" serious

eyestrain

47%	office workers
30%	top executives
43%	facilities managers
interior designers	89%

quality of air

37%	office workers
25%	top executives
31%	facilities managers
interior designers	84%

When [Xerox PARC anthropologist] Lucy Schuman asked [accounting] clerks to describe their jobs, their descriptions corresponded more or less to the formal procedures of the job manual. But when she observed them at work, she discovered that the clerks…instead relied on a rich variety of informal practices that weren't in any manual but turned out to be crucial to getting the work done. In fact, the clerks were constantly improvising, inventing new methods to deal with unexpected difficulties and to solve immediate problems. Without being aware of it, they were far more innovative and creative than anybody who heard them describe their "routine" jobs ever would have thought…. If local innovation is as important and pervasive as we expect, then big companies have the potential to be remarkably innovative —*if* they can somehow capture that innovation and learn from it.

John Seely Brown, "Research That Reinvents the Corporation," *Harvard Business Review*, Jan/Feb 1991

work & play

average number of working hours and vacation days in major international cities

City	Work	Play
Istanbul	57.8	23.6
Hong Kong	52.0	7.6
Seoul	50.8	20.2
Mexico City	45.4	10.1
Singapore	44.0	17.2
Tokyo	43.0	16.1
AVERAGE	42.3	20.9
Chicago	41.5	10.9
Houston	41.2	14.1
Geneva	40.9	23.7
Los Angeles	40.5	14.2
New York	39.7	13.0
Frankfurt	39.5	29.5
Paris	38.8	28.2
Sydney	38.5	20.0
London	38.3	24.1
Brussels	37.3	24.3

This brings up a point about the crumbling of this false-front hierarchy. What's the reward of rising in an organization if one is faced with isolation rather than influence? The corporate pyramids are flattening because companies have learned that they work better when people share rather than withhold information and when they stay in close contact with the public. Business consultants began to encourage nomadic management. How effective can you be if you're away from the action?

Regardless of official guidelines, policies, and pronouncements, effective office workers will develop "guerilla layouts" to thwart an office design that inhibits them from performing well. **Why not incorporate their successes?** Good work should indeed be rewarded, and if that means a corner office and dark wood panelling, so be it. **But keep this in mind: the office plan should be integral to the business, not a grid laid over an organization chart.**

MYTH 2: People who do the same function should be grouped together.

This is the reverse of Myth 1, where people who had nothing in common except salary level were grouped together on "Mahogany Row." Myth 2 applies to the "little people:" The popular assumption of management (who, after all, has been locked away on some remote floor like Sleeping Beauty in her weed-choked castle) has been that the "people" in accounting couldn't possibly benefit from being close to the sales department, the operations group, the customer service people, or, heaven forbid, the executive cadre.

"Similitude breeds efficiency" is another way of stating this myth. It dates back to grade school, when all the "good" readers were segregated from the lesser lights in the classroom, or to high school, when those enrolled in "college prep" courses didn't cross the "vocational training" line. Somehow people got the notion that things work best when we sit with the people whose skills and interests most closely resemble our own. This idea is so absurd—even on the surface—that it's hard to understand how it ever took hold other than for the obvious reason of control, which is really the issue. In other words, grouping everyone who has the same job title together makes the group easier to supervise, even if the cost is reducing the overall value of the work and the worker.

Think about it on a personal level. Is there anything to be learned from a person who knows one thing? It's impossible to imagine listening to such a bore. Of course physical resources

radiation from VDTs		repetitive strain injury		hazardous materials	
36%	office workers	**33%**	office workers	**19%**	office workers
24%	top executives	**28%**	top executives	**12%**	top executives
22%	facilities managers	**21%**	facilities managers	**17%**	facilities managers
interior designers	**75%**	**interior designers**	**71%**	**interior designers**	**71%**

OEI Survey 1991

should be shared; there's no need for expensive **redundancy.** But if it makes sense to have all the accountants grouped together because they all use the same file cabinets and reference material, don't assume that completes the picture of what these people need to do a good job for the company.

Imagine an incredibly effective salesperson. She may have learned technique from a customer service representative, who in turn admires the skill of the courteous office receptionist, who in turn models herself after the professionalism of the director of research, who respects the ability of the office librarian, who readily acknowledges that most information is not written down, and therefore makes a point of talking every day to the mailperson, who is in touch with the entire organization.

Good work is about knowledge gained and well-applied, in addition to skills repeated and refined. To be effective, an office plan has to recognize the **potential** of the people in the office and not simply pay attention to the lowest common denominator of job descriptions.

MYTH 3: **Coffee rooms, drinking fountains, and lunchrooms are, at best, wasted space and, at worst, an open invitation to poor work habits and overall laxity.**

This is the ugly side of the **Protestant work ethic;** the corporate extension of H.L. Mencken's definition of a puritan as the person who worries that someone, somewhere, is having a good time. The corollary to this is that if something's enjoyable, it must not be work.

Such thinking demonstrates a manager's grim lack of faith in the maturity and sense of **responsibility** of the office staff. It begs the question of whether any one employee has value to the entire organization. Denying the richness of conversational interchange is like pricing an organization at 50% of its book value! A business is not made up of departments and divisions, it's made up of people, and the knowledge these people have and share is every bit as valuable as the $10 million mainframe in the $2 million computer room—and a lot easier to get at.

Good conversation breeds good ideas, and serendipitous conversation breeds the best ideas of all. It's really not necessary to worry about the square feet begrudgingly allotted to the lunchroom or the tedious placement of vending machines and coffee stations every 500 feet. What matters is a frame of mind that encourages interchange rather than resenting a 10-minute break from routine. Of course, the majority of such conversations are about what was on television last night and other such personal gossip, but even that has its value. These

Work should be set up "without the necessity of the clerk even rising from his seat...for where the work does not flow in this manner there is a constant tendency for clerks to do their own messenger work.... It should not be overlooked that while a clerk is not at his desk he may be working, but he is not doing clerical work effectively."

William Henry Leffingwell, *Office Management: Principles and Practices*, 1925

Business is a good game—lots of competition and a minimum of rules. You keep score with money.

Attributed to Atari founder Nolan Bushnell

Work is half one's life—and the other half, too.

Erich Kastner

people have to work together; doesn't it make sense they should be encouraged to get along? We've seen the rather dramatic collapse of mind control everywhere else in the world. If people trust each other enough to discuss childrearing techniques, perhaps they can be thrown together on a task force with tight deadlines for developing a new product or a better delivery system.

People spend their lives trying to improve the obvious and do things easier, faster, and better. If such energy exists on a personal level—and it clearly does—then surely a company can only benefit by channeling and challenging that energy to business needs.

Breaks are important. Conversation is important. It's the only way to find out for sure who the experts really are.

MYTH 4: The office is a place to escape from; the home is a place to escape to.

Some readers of this book may have been working long enough to remember the plastic and primary-color era of offices in the late '60s and early '70s. And these cheery bits of red, yellow, and blue were actually improvements over the gunmetal grey of the preceding 20 years.

The thinking was that offices should be as crisp, clean, sharp, modern, clutter-free, and antiseptic as possible. Home, on the other hand, was a place comfortably loaded up with faux antiques, wood-grain paneling, deep-pile carpeting, and all the trappings of **traditionalism.**

A funny thing happened on the way to the 21st century. The office crept into the house and personal life crept into the office. The reason Myth 4 can't be sustained is the most obvious of all: nothing in life is that simple.

Offices are populated by the same people who live in houses, condos, apartments, houseboats, and trailers. These people are men and women; some are parents, some are grandparents; many are married, many are not. A significant number might not have English as a first language. Many went to college, more did not. And yet the assumption has always been that a clean, impersonal office will act as the great leveler to get productive work out of all these people. With all these needs and skills, certainly it makes better sense to design an office that has a range of furnishing and layout options, a variety with some logic to it. Such options should exist not to accommodate personal whim but to recognize practical reality.

As office hours stretch from 6 AM to 9 PM (or later), increasing numbers of people find the distinction between home and office blurred. A visit to many a "tasteful" professional

couple's home in the '80s would have revealed starker blacks and whites (and more technology) than many small offices could dream of. For someone whose office is also his or her home, the two spaces don't even have to be furnished differently...they can each be furnished to the person's needs, interests, and taste. The spaces don't have to be separated by a hallway, a floor, or even a solid wall.

The truth is, with faxes, overnight delivery, car phones, and voice mail, the only thing that keeps a home from turning into an office is sheer willpower.

The office environment, on the other hand, is finding that it must adapt to the pressing needs of a variable workforce. As soon as the paralyzing rigidity of an office organized by blueprints is let go, a business grants itself the **freedom** to be organized, designed, and furnished in the ways that contribute most to its overall success.

Making an office comfortable is not soft management; it's a highly effective tool for employee recruitment and retention—not to mention making workers more productive.

MYTH 5: You will perform best when you look and act like everybody else.

For years, American business operated like a manufacturing plant. We shake our heads at the blue lab coats that all the employees wear at Toyota plants, but don't think to question our own grey flannel suit pandemic. Japanese workers wear the same clothes to reinforce the concept of the equal value of every employee; perhaps we adopted the grey flannel suit as a reflection of our belief in the strength of our manufacturing economy —recognizing the equality of workers had nothing to do with it. Everything (people included) became a commodity; as long as

Dress for success?

There are millions and millions of people who are self-employed and work in small businesses, who love the fact that they get up in the morning and don't have to dress for success.

Paul Hawken, founder of Smith and Hawken, a successful US company whose merchandise includes casual clothing.

Consider the Source:

American executives, by an eight-to-one margin, are adopting more casual dress, yet the vast majority of them favor decorative over utilitarian furnishings, according to two recent surveys. The studies were conducted, respectively, by athletic-shoe manufacturer Converse Inc. and Art Specialty Co., a maker of decorative lamps.

Wall Street Journal, September 24, 1991

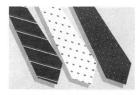

The Ties that Bind

Because suits are mandatory for so many businessmen, ties have become an outlet of self-expression, creativity, and diversity. While some think they are bucking the trend with a simple yellow tie (possibly with paisleys), others find beautiful, unique works of art that are anything but loud or crazy.

profile of heavy computer users

charts compare all office workers to heavy computer users (hcu's)

by job description

	all	hcu's
managerial	39%	23%
professional/technical	32%	36%
clerical/secretarial	26%	40%

by gender

	all	hcu's
female	54%	66%
male	46%	34%

all	all office workers
hcu's	heavy computer user

Moving forward is worse than standing still.

Winston Churchill

John Seely Brown, the director of Xerox's Palo Alto Research Center, describes a radical departure from the usual focus on making copiers perfect: "We proposed an alternative approach to design. Instead of trying to eliminate 'trouble,' we acknowledged that it was inevitable." Instead of being designed to "not break down," the new copiers are designed to be helpful *when* they break down, so they are easier for customers to fix quickly and get on with their work.

is your boss listening to you?

importance of management encouraging a free exchange of information among employees and departments

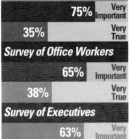

75%	Very Important
35%	Very True

Survey of Office Workers

65%	Very Important
38%	Very True

Survey of Executives

63%	Very Important
35%	Very True

Survey of Facility Managers

OEI Survey 1989

---

the overall quality remained high, individual performance was not important.

Well, for better or worse, we now live in an era of specialization, acutely discriminating customers, and hairline competitive edges. **Innovation** is not popular as a mere consultant toss-off, it's essential to survival. Innovation is just another term for evolution and, as in nature, the strong and smart will survive and thrive.

The point is not to advocate mayhem in the office; it makes sense to have the entire office send a coherent message about the business, but the message shouldn't be left to whim or "correct thinking." From the reception area to the mailroom, the work areas, and the executive offices every space should have a meaning and all the meanings should tie in to the company's purpose. So should the appearance and behavior of the employees.

If the office communicates a coherent message for the staff, the customers, and the business, then having a message is probably a good idea. It may even be that the entire office has a dress code—certainly it seems that way in the design industry, where every entry-level designer is issued black clothes and a ponytail. This is no different from Thomas Watson's crisp white shirts at IBM. And the communication of the message, whether of studied separateness or corporate fraternity, is equally inescapable.

If, however, the business imposes structure for reasons of control rather than coherence and employees are not allowed to understand the thinking behind certain rules, then the chances of this being a living, breathing, dynamic business are slim.

Everything is a message, intended or not; a powerful business is one that shapes the message to its own purposes.

MYTH 6: Innovation is fine for some businesses, but others can't afford change.

This is the myth of the puny payoff, otherwise known as the **short-term gain.** Gigantic publishing companies, which stand the most to gain, have cautiously and reluctantly tiptoed into the bracing waters of electronic publishing. The **cost** of junking the existing systems (and it's symptomatic of this way of thinking that everything has to be all one way or all the other!) is "too high." Would anyone care to guess what the cost of resurrecting a business from the dead is? The reverse is just as frequent; someone comes up with a great "money-saving idea" for a nonexistent problem, but since the technology

by personal income

	all	hcu's
$35,000 or less	57%	71%
over $35,000	37%	22%

by education

	all	hcu's
less than college grad	55%	62%
college grad or more	45%	38%

by size of organization

	all	hcu's
100 or less	12%	12%
101–500	17%	13%
501–5,000	25%	27%
over 5,000	34%	34%

OEI Survey 1991

exists, it must be necessary to acquire. This is how most companies seem to buy their phone systems.

It's all too common for people to patch together bad ideas and make do, because the pervasive fear is that doing something right **once** is much more expensive than doing things wrong in increments. It's the story about the manufacturer who lost a dollar on every sale, but planned to make up for it in volume.

With office planning, it's not always necessary, or even advisable, to have a master plan sandwiched between Plexiglas and mounted on the wall for everyone to see. A business must commit to the "what" of its office design and accept that the "how" will change from time to time. This keeps the business from being trapped by invalid thinking. A philosopher, when challenged that he had changed his mind on an issue, said, "Formerly, I was not as wise as I am now." It's true for anyone who pays attention to what goes on around him or her.

For a change to be valuable, it does not have to guarantee a dollar-for-dollar return on investment, or a dollar-for-dollar gain over the previous idea. A change should not be random or isolated. Change is disruptive; if it is to be proposed and implemented, it must have worth. An individual change should not stand or fall on its own merit, rather it should be considered in the context of the ultimate goal.

Change, in other words, is a means, not an end.

Some designers (and bosses, too) believe that a space should be clean and uncluttered—almost sterile—so that the office is a nonintrusive stage in which the color and life are provided by the people and activities in it.

Most corporate marketing and communications divisions now have a better understanding of electronic publishing (and therefore more powerful tools) than any of the big publishing houses in New York City. Where market-driven types see an edge, the entrenched see a threat or, worse, an expense.

The success of a small firm's strategic plan is often contingent on the information used to create the plan. A firm that can scan and react to trends in its external environment is most likely to succeed. The information itself is often personal, or experience-based, rather than institutional, and this, too, appears to be significant in a changing, fluid business environment.

Pamela Hammers Specht, "Information Sources Used for Strategic Planning Decisions in Small Firms," *American Journal of Small Business* (Spring 1987)

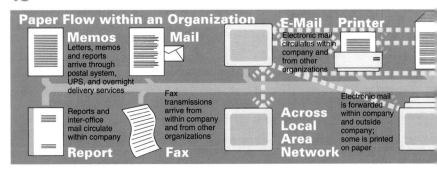

Paper Flow within an Organization

Memos
Letters, memos and reports arrive through postal system, UPS, and overnight delivery services

Mail

E-Mail
Electronic mail circulates within company and from other organizations

Printer

Report
Reports and inter-office mail circulate within company

Fax
Fax transmissions arrive from within company and from other organizations

Across Local Area Network

Electronic mail is forwarded within company and outside company; some is printed on paper

One of the hottest topics in business performance in the '80s was "customer service"—from customer contact to quality of goods. Catching on in the '90s is the realization that employees who feel valued in turn treat customers and product as valued, sweeping out rigid pyramid structures and hierarchies of communication, and bringing in "empowerment," "open doors" (or no doors), and "management by walking around."

Design from the inside out. First design the process and the players, then talk about the tools.

Wayne D. Veneklasen, psychologist and manager of facility planning at Steelcase, Inc.

Fail to honor people,
They fail to honor you;
But of a good leader,
who talks little,
When his work is done,
his aim fulfilled,
They will all say,
"We did this ourselves."

Lao Tzu

PERFORMANCE

Designing for Performance

It's interesting that myths about the office are mostly myths about **office culture;** they have to do with how people relate to and understand one another. The six myths cited above have to do with people and their need to judge **performance,** maintain **power,** and establish **proximity.** These needs confirm the suspicion that, more than anything else, office design is about relationships. A successful office is one that gives credence and coherence to these concerns.

The overriding concern in any business should be performance. Performance has many meanings. The obvious business definition for performance is **bottom line return**—but how many "rehearsals" precede the smash hit "performance" of financial success? Clearly the performance of the staff and the performance of the product or service provided by the staff are the critical components of success.

Performance is the art of function. The science of function is figuring out what things cost, looking at reports and statistics, doing market research, establishing tangible goals, and so forth. The art of function is getting people to do the things they need to do for the business to succeed. A plan is not enough.

These days employees assess the performance of a business and an office, as critically as they themselves are reviewed. How well does the office work? How does the office contribute to personal and professional **employee satisfaction?** How does the office assist the productivity level of the employee? Managers and office planners should ask similar questions: What's the real worth of the office design? (Hint: It's *not*

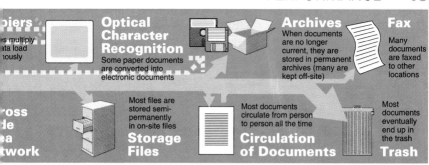

Optical Character Recognition
Some paper documents are converted into electronic documents

Archives
When documents are no longer current, they are stored in permanent archives (many are kept off-site)

Fax
Many documents are faxed to other locations

Most files are stored semi-permanently in on-site files

Storage Files

Most documents circulate from person to person all the time

Circulation of Documents

Most documents eventually end up in the trash

Trash

the amount of money saved, but the potential for revenue earned.) Is office design looked upon as a cost or an investment? The answer to this question reveals the opinion a company has of its employees as well as the long-term likelihood of this business's survival.

To think about office design in terms of performance, think about what's needed for a job to be done well. Don't limit the thinking to equipment; it's not enough. On a simple level, people perform best when they are **comfortable and secure.** We don't mean the false security of an entrenched bureaucracy—that's inertia, not security, and we don't mean the comfort of having eight hours to do four hours' worth of work. We're talking about the comfort and security of **belonging,** of knowing your work matters—and that you'll hear about it when you fall behind as well as when you come out ahead. The comforts an employee needs are, in our opinion, fairly simple to provide: **good ventilation, adequate light, equipment that's appropriate to the work, an office culture that encourages involvement, and room enough to store things.** It's possible that a business cannot afford the latest (and most expensive) ergonomically designed furniture and screen guards for PCs. Fine—compensate by encouraging employees to move around a bit, shift to other tasks, offer to help somewhere else for a while. Few business owners actually own the buildings that house their offices and therefore cannot completely control the heating and ventilation—but, again, employees could go outside occasionally for a breath of fresh air or be encouraged to dress comfortably for the season. Certainly many offices have outright banned certain noxious acts such as smoking in closed spaces.

There is a Middle Eastern (and somewhat dated) proverb about a father with a rather plain daughter of marriageable age. Nobody will take her off his hands—or offer even the most meager bride price. Finally, a suitor comes along who offers 10 cows. The father is astounded at the offer, but, of course, accepts it—feeling rather sorry for his foolish future son-in-law. In fact, the girl blossoms in the marriage and turns out to be radiantly beautiful and a terrific wife. The moral being: treat people like they're worth 10 cows and they will be. If you want the best possible performance, give every indication that you think it's possible. And don't assume you know everything. Sometimes it takes a new pair of eyes to see.

POWER

If performance is the weathervane, then power might be the wind. It doesn't much matter how much wind is blown if it's blowing in the wrong direction or summoned at the wrong time.

Power is a weighted-down word; it carries a lot of baggage. One frequently hears about the "trappings of power." The origin of this phrase is the ornamental coverings for a horse (blankets, saddles, bridles, etc.), but it's interesting to see how "trap" is so much a part of this. An office doesn't exude power because of its physical objects. If you walk into the Oval Office, you're overwhelmed by the presence of power, not by the rug of the great seal on the floor. In fact, many of the icons associated with power are not really power symbols at all; they're simply **status symbols** that say "I've been here 25 years," "My uncle owns the company," or "I earn $300,000 per year." Furnishings provide powerful clues and help to establish some sort of framework for the kind of person who occupies the space, but power itself? No.

Conversation with John Sculley, CEO of Apple Computer, Inc.

OfficeAccess talked to as well-known a person as there is in American industry, and here's what he told us about the design of his office:

OA: *You were trained in architecture; what did that training have to do with this office? How did you decide to have this little, tiny office?*

JS: First of all, I decided my office wouldn't be my business card, an icon of my position. Second, Apple is in a constant state of change—in fact, change is really the fuel of

Apple. So, as people have to move around frequently, I wanted to negate the idea that there was any status attached to having a certain kind of office. I decided my office would be smaller and less prestigious than that of anybody who worked for me.

The next thing I decided was that, for me, an office did not have to connote power, but it ought to connote what I do. This is really form follows function. I meet with people in conversation, so a round table works for me; there really is no sense of any one individual being more important than another.

I do a lot of teamwork with three or four people, so the round table is an important icon for me.

I also work a lot with technology. I need access to technology; it's not an ornament for me, but an extension of what I do. So if I do electronic mail, I'm over here; if I want to check in on communications—what's going on with the high-technology industry, I'm over there; if I want to watch a video, I'm over here.

Technology is very much integrated into the way I work; technology tools are the things that work successfully for me. There are some things that **don't** work successfully in this office. For instance, the organization of things, unfortunately, is not very successful here. Stuff is stacked up and nothing really seems to fit in the right place—things like that. So things could be a lot better.

I tend to read a lot, so there are books all over the place. But reading is a transference for me, so books come in, I grab a bunch and read them and bring them back—or maybe I never bring them back. The bookshelves are a holding space/area for me. My office isn't terribly personalized. It's not designed for show. There are a lot of things that are terrible about it: the

The power to be your best.

The office as icon

Inventory of a boss's office:

A typical office of a chief executive or partner may contain some or all of the following "trappings of power":

Top floor (if the company occupies a tall building)

Corner location

Windows

Door that locks

Luxurious adjacent reception area equipped with a secretary as guardian

Original works of art

Photographs of the boss with the President of the US, other business leaders, and family

Professional awards

Golf trophies

Persian rug and/or wool carpet

Leather chair—throne-like in design to signify the "seat of power"

Wood furniture

Expensive finishes such as marble, brass, and stainless steel

Rare plants

Exotic fish aquarium

Private washroom

Fireplace

Built-in bar

lighting is awful, the heat is terrible, there's no privacy. There are a lot of things I'd do differently.

OA: *Would you have more privacy?*

JS: Well, actually, I would be happier in a cube because there's more privacy in a cube than in a cage.

It shouldn't come as any surprise that Apple's slogan is "The power to be your best." Power has meaning only when it's put to use, and has value only when that use serves a positive end. On the world stage we have seen over and again the challenge that the power of freedom presents to the temporary power of suppression. Power without support is merely force; and since force makes people miserable and relies on fear and helplessness to be sustained, it takes some doing to overcome—but instance after instance shows that power does finally assert itself. The power a business needs to succeed is this kind of power—the power to lead.

The real "trappings" of power are knowledge, clearheadedness, conviction, accessibility, and understanding. How an office design accommodates these qualities is a measure of the kind of power afoot in that office. The most salient feature of real power is that it's comfortable with itself; a CEO who has built a company or rescued it from financial collapse or successfully followed through a much-needed change should certainly be comfortable with rewarding himself or herself with the personal office of his or her choosing. And again, that's another aspect of power: choice. Power is the ability to make distinctions and intelligent choices. It would be a foolish leader (and office designer) who, in a burst of egalitarianism, decided everyone in the office should have exactly the same kind of work space. This mistaken concept of "power" disrupts the real need people have for recognition and the real differences in the ways people work. What should be the same throughout the office are the standards against which one is judged, not the rewards for the performance itself.

Office design should address the issue of power as one of business performance, not as a matter of personal control. Certainly, business behavior has trended this way in the past 50 years. The model for the Eisenhower era was the adult-child relationship. The parent/boss had all the "power" (which was really only the power to demand and suppress), and the children/workers showed up, did what they were told, and went home to mom. The early '70s evidenced a persuasion-based relationship that mirrored the adult/young adult concerns of the time. Manag rs tried to accommodate by persuasion—"Let's just give it a ·y"—implying that it would only be a matter of time before the mployee grew to see things the way the boss did. Currently, we ·re in a peer-to-peer era, influenced by the expectations of the ·orkforce and the reality that many employees are as technically ompetent, or more so, than their supervisors. Such a relation-·hip can go one of two ways: the path of tension and resentment ·r the path of **acknowledgment** and recognition. A man-·ger who resents an employee's skill and an employee who re-·ents a manager's judgment don't stand much of a chance, and ·he vacuum created by an empowerment opportunity will be ·lled either by force or anarchy. The results may not be as cata-·trophic as political collapse, but they will still be devastating to a ·articular business.

So we acknowledge the real place for power in the office · in empowerment. Everyone moves in the same direction, ·ut each makes the contribution that makes the best use of his or ·er skills. It's an ideal; no one assumes such a situation can sud-·enly just appear in the office scene.

In fact, part of a manager's fear of having a "responsive" ·ffice plan is that employees would make unreasonable re-·uests. But imagine truly having the "power to do your best." ·Vhat would that take? If everyone in the office agreed to articu-·te personal needs in terms of the business, the company ·ould be effectively channeled to support the business. The ··pe of "demands" made on the office design would, in fact, ·e the type most likely to be implemented. One aspect of ·ower is recognizing its worth, its place, and its timing. An ·ffice plan built on giving people the best **opportunity** to ·erform is truly a powerful tool.

Blue and white collars have apparently had their day. The latest collar is gold. Gold collars are the irreplaceable professionals who command high salaries and ample job security for their knowledge and skill. The best computer programmers, financial service experts, and anyone who's a year or two ahead of commonly understood technology fall into this category, which, significantly, does not include traditional management.

Bigelow
FINE CARPET SINCE 1825

"A name on the door rates a Bigelow on the floor."

Ad from Bigelow Carpet Company, circa 1955

Most are engaged in business the greater part of their lives because the soul abhors a vacuum and they have not discovered any continuous employment for men's nobler faculties.

Henry David Thoreau, 1954

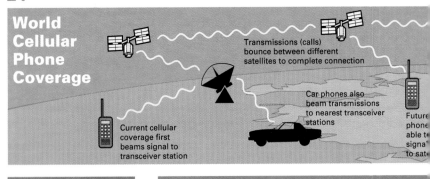

World Cellular Phone Coverage

Transmissions (calls) bounce between different satellites to complete connection

Car phones also beam transmissions to nearest transceiver stations

Current cellular coverage first beams signal to transceiver station

Future phone able to signa' to sate

141 square feet (1991)

The average office space per worker amounts to just under 150 square feet.

What many office workers prefer:

1. A single entrance to a workstation

2. Some enclosure for visual and acoustic privacy

3. Having at least two work surfaces in the workspace

4. For managers, having a work surface that permits face-to-face, across-the-desk conversation

What many office workers don't prefer:

1. Other people seated at work directly in front of them

2. A workstation with open sides facing directly onto an aisle that many people use

PROXIMITY

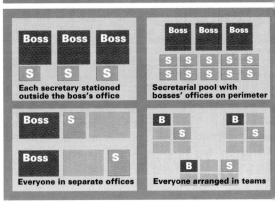

Boss **Boss** **Boss**
S S S
Each secretary stationed outside the boss's office

Boss **Boss** **Boss**
S S S S S
S S S S S
Secretarial pool with bosses' offices on perimeter

Boss S
Boss S
Everyone in separate offices

B B
S S
B S
Everyone arranged in teams

Proximity is the most personal of the people issues in an office. Performance is a way of judging the individual in terms c the business; power is fraught with social implications; proximity has to do with the space one inhabits.

Proximity can certainly be a function of either power performance. There is a message about power, or perhaps mor accurately of position, in the placement of a secretary close enough to be within calling distance of a boss. There is a message in the space allowed to one level of employee versus that allowed to another. And proximity is certainly a performance is sue, because the convenience of access to people and resource affects the work you do.

The cost of things bears significantly on proximity. Space costs, for instance, are a significant portion of any business budget; so are people and the equipment they use. An office design cannot assume that the money available to suppo it is limitless. Personal proximity needs, therefore, must be balanced against what the business requires and what the busines will pay to have such needs met.

If fitting a certain number of people into a fixed amount c space is a given, what steps can be taken to assure that maximum performance within that space is achieved? First, a space planner or facilities manager should check his or her plans against the expectations of those affected by the plans. A dialogue doesn't mean a wholesale revision is in store; it may b that no revision at all will be made—but communication is as much a part, indeed a much greater part, of office design than are furniture purchasing and placement.

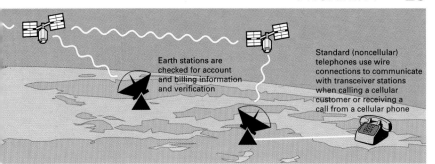

Earth stations are checked for account and billing information and verification

Standard (noncellular) telephones use wire connections to communicate with transceiver stations when calling a cellular customer or receiving a call from a cellular phone

The concerns people have about proximity are probably fairly common sense ones. Each of these concerns can be addressed in a reasonable, performance-oriented office plan.

People Like Face-To-Face Contact

Despite advances in telecommunications, despite the home office, and despite the phenomena of departmentalization and **compartmentalization** of offices, proximity is a value in and of itself. Most people need to move about, see other people, talk to colleagues. Since people are social creatures, it goes against their nature to inhibit social contact. Many subtle, important, and productive cues occur between two or more people in person that don't occur over phone lines or via e-mail.

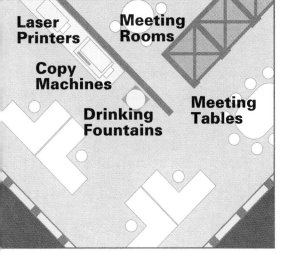

Laser Printers

Meeting Rooms

Copy Machines

Drinking Fountains

Meeting Tables

It's a good thing to be placed near the people you deal with most regularly, but there's a value, too, in bumping into a new employee or a person whose office is down the hall. An office can plan for such encounters by designing spaces that are easily accessible to one another. Paths can weave among work spaces without being intrusive. Panel heights can meet both privacy and conversation needs. An office plan can be sprinkled with alternate work spaces: a cluster of chairs, a meeting room, open space near the windows. Giving an employee a feeling of **movement** and openness allows the feeling to be used to good advantage.

The costs of running an office: Minimum amount of space for a private office is 96 sq. ft.—that's about 8' x 12'. The minimum area for a workstation is about 64 sq. ft., about 8' x 8' or even smaller. If you have an office space of 10,000 sq. ft., assume that 15% goes for circulation and support spaces. The remaining 8,500 sq. ft. will provide 132 workstations of 64 sq. ft. each as opposed to only 88 private offices at 96 sq. ft. each, i.e., 50% more spaces.

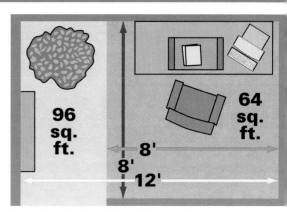

space glut?

average work space per worker and average cost per square foot in U.S. downtown areas

City	Sq Ft/Wkr	Cost/SqFt
San Antonio	393	$9.08
Dallas	385	$16.05
Houston	347	$12.89
New Orleans	257	$9.19
Seattle	271	$16.86
Washington, DC	314	$27.96
Atlanta	317	$13.14
Salt Lake City	292	$11.57
Portland, OR	291	$13.87
Phoenix	315	$12.99
Cleveland	310	$11.73
Birmingham	276	$12.43
Pittsburgh	267	$20.95
Jacksonville	270	$16.65
Denver	282	$10.64
Chicago	284	$22.53
San Francisco	295	$23.45
Los Angeles	279	$22.36
Boston	231	$20.30
Philadelphia	257	$18.79
New York City	248	$31.30
Sacramento	274	$21.88
Milwaukee	289	$17.25
Hartford	239	$24.12
Buffalo	221	$12.91
Charlotte	257	$14.77
Columbus, OH	275	$15.10
Honolulu	233	$28.33
Baltimore	238	$19.47
Detroit	328	$15.38
Indianapolis	245	$14.42
Minneapolis	265	$19.66

Source: 1992 Experience Exchange Report, Building Owners and Managers Association International

Practically Speaking, Proximity Equals Convenience

Proximity is about access. Are the things and people you need to work well nearby? In a small office, **convenience** seems like it should be a given. Everything *is* in one place, but then helpful tools for organization, and courteous and intelligent use of space become paramount. In a larger office, there may be some trade-off between an individual's desire to have immediate proximity to certain resources (copy rooms, supply cabinets, shared computer terminals) versus the greater need of the greater numbers. Obviously, if there is only one fax machine, someone will be closest to it. Such placement decisions are based on highest use, as well as on practical matters such as noise and sightlines. But placement decisions must also be made with informed **understanding** of the value of people and tools. Secretaries are not merely automatons who crank out form letters. They have probably the richest understanding of what is happening anywhere in the office. Likewise, a **fax machine** is not merely an electronic-mail deliverer—it has become a vital office communications link. Banishing it to a closet is like cutting off your ear.

Proximity Should Relate to Workflow

In almost any office a **variety** of tasks are performed. Not only do the end results of these tasks differ (delivering a report, for example, versus mailing a check), the **work patterns** required to accomplish these tasks will vary. Proximity should take into account the way that work flows through an office. **Independent tasks,** even in a large office, are those that one person can accomplish. Sorting and delivering mail (if

...he volume isn't crushing) and answering the main telephone ...re examples of jobs that are handled in relative isolation; other ...obs are **repetitive** in nature but, because of the volume of ...vork, several people perform the same function: word-process-...ng pools, telemarketers, and insurance-claims processors are ...xamples of these kinds of workers. It seems reasonable to seat ...hese people together since they can help one another perform ...heir tasks (allowing, however, for breaks from routine—both ...ocial and visual).

Independent Workflow

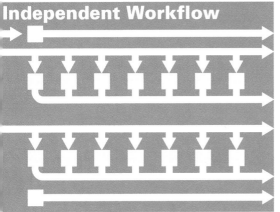

Other work is done **sequentially.** Accounting depart-...ments often work this way. Someone opens, dates, and routes ...n invoice; another person researches the invoice and attaches it ...o project-related information; a third person reviews the in-...oice, approves or rejects it, and accounts for it in a project bud-...et; and a fourth person actually signs the check. The process

Sequential Workflow

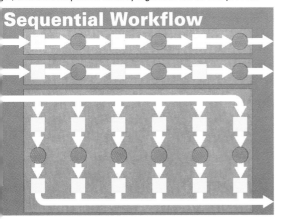

The new SATURN auto plant in Tennessee pays more than lip service to the idea that the workers make the company successful—each employee has free access to all the company's financial information and is both empowered and encouraged to make cost-saving suggestions and improvements. In keeping with the corporate belief in the worth of the employees, each work team has its own conference room furnished with a computer linked to the rest of the company, filing cabinets whose color the team chooses, and the same padded chairs that the company president has in his or her own office.

In his book *Neuromancer*, William Gibson describes corporations as the highest form of life on this planet.

personal space
preferred office arrangements of workers

Arrangement	Percent	Year
	61%	1989
	65%	1988
Private		
	23%	1989
	23%	1988
Partitioned		
	14%	1989
	11%	1988
Open Space		

OEI Survey 1989

Elements that promote privacy

Glass Blocks   Glass Walls   Doo

Personal Distances

There are hierarchies of proximity: *Intimate* indicates the closest personal relations, such as those between parents and children and loved ones. *Personal* contacts are 1:1 conversational relationships. *Social* means contacts at parties, business meetings, and conferences, with more than two people typically involved. *Public* contacts occur between a speaker and an audience, i.e. a teacher and class.

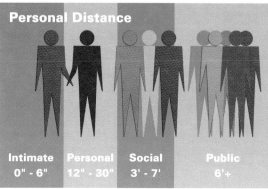

Personal Distance

Intimate	Personal	Social	Public
0" - 6"	12" - 30"	3' - 7'	6'+

may work in reverse for receivables. Clearly it's important for these people to be near each other, but it may also be important to be close to other workers whose information and decisions are part of the process. Who ordered the work, for example, and is the data-processing department running checks today? Is this vendor an approved vendor? Is the price fair? And so on.

Sequential work once modelled itself on the **assembly line.** Everybody was responsible for a part, but nobody was responsible for the whole. Effective sequential work these days is **circular**—everyone involved in the process acts as a quality-control check on everyone else. Their space should be designed with quality-control tools in mind rather than for the isolated steps of incremental progress.

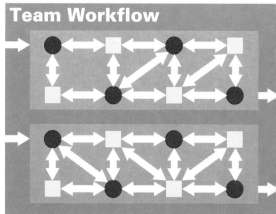

Team Workflow

The need for proximity may be greatest in an office with a lot of **team workflow**—which resembles the sequential workflow except that every individual has multiple responsibili-

lant Screens   Partitions   Banners

This scene from an office meeting tells a story of the three P's **(proximity, performance, power)** in action: The scene takes place in the conference room of an office. The senior manager is clearly in control of the meeting, given the attentive looks of the staff, most of whom lean forward or toward the manager so as to hear every point being made. The meeting leader appears comfortable in his or her position of control. Our assumption is that the directives and decisions issued at this meeting will be quickly and decisively acted upon.

Clustered Workstations

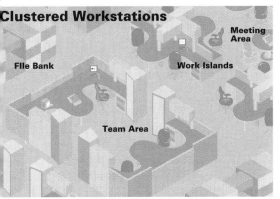

File Bank   Work Islands   Meeting Area

Team Area

es. Perhaps this is most common in small businesses. At the **Understanding**Business, the design director is also the project manager and the production manager; editors are also responsible for contracts; the people who make the maps also lay out the books; and the proofreaders are also fact-checkers and contributors to the text. Nearly everyone who works in an editorial capacity is also computer-design literate. With so much cross responsibility, proximity isn't a courtesy, it's a necessity. With no spare hands, everyone must be able to know at a glance what everyone else is working on. This avoids redundancy and encourages the sharing that underlies efficiency.

Proximity and Privacy

This is a thorny issue in office design. Nearly everyone would like more space and the opportunity to occasionally shut oneself away. Historically, both in the office and in social life, privacy has been associated with position and the ability to afford the luxury of "extra" space. Privacy is a subjective (but

One popular way of providing privacy in an office while letting natural light enter is the glass wall. These walls are usually soundproof when sound privacy is necessary but afford an open atmosphere.

nonetheless real) need; therefore no office design, however well intentioned, can hope to satisfy everyone's privacy needs. It helps to know, however, that there are varying degrees of privacy and varying solutions to the problems that privacy poses. What most people need in an office is **temporary privacy** to make a sensitive phone call or to have a face-to-face meeting or to work on a demanding project. Even the smallest office should make some effort to meet this need with a set-off space or enclosed meeting room. Some businesses have privacy at their essence: a law office, a medical practice, a research lab. These professionals need to ensure the privacy of their information, their customers, or both. In such offices, privacy is a corporate rather than personal issue and office designs may include not only a significant number of individual offices, but elaborate **security measures,** as well. These measures (employee identification, door passes, signout sheets, and the like) are intended to keep the company's information private. They also act as a deterrent from too much private contact between employees. Individual businesses should determine the extent to which the need for corporate privacy supplants the need for personal privacy.

Research and design facilities often take elaborate, expensive and contradictory measures to make employees feel comfortable, although they're under **surveillance.** We've found that despite the effort put into atriums, lunchrooms, breakaway spaces, and the like, employees are disinclined to take advantage of these opportunities for withdrawal or quiet conversation because security measures are clearly the overriding concern. Since people are rarely fooled by "the iron fist in the velvet glove," perhaps companies should rethink the expense of these mutually exclusive efforts.

Personal Privacy

People are amazingly resilient. The best office plans try to understand people, but, of course, that's a continually elusive challenge. People, therefore, have devised their own ways of dealing with proximity and privacy issues because the variability of the workforce demands it. No office plan can deal with the whistler, the person who reads other people's mail, the gum snapper, and the opinionated loudmouth all at once. People instead devise mechanisms of etiquette and exclusion to keep some aspect of their work lives private. Don't ask us what they do. It's simply important to recognize that when it comes to privacy, people will deal with the issue as they best know how—and it is not necessary for an office plan to do more than acknowledge that no one solution works for every situation.

There is one final issue concerning proximity, and that is doing without it. Working at home means opting out of day-to-day and face-to-face interaction, but it can also increase the value of other **"approximate" proximities.** When you work at home, you really have to rely on technology. You need to know how your computer works, when the post office closes, the filing dates for business taxes, and much much more. People who work at home or run independent businesses need intimate knowledge about things the rest of us can get from somebody else. Home workers should also be great telephone callers; they need to make an extra effort to stay in touch, so every conversation should be meaningful and interesting. Finally, only the most misanthropic (and least successful!) of these workers can avoid office contact for long. They inevitably show up for meetings or to share resources and, in doing so, powerfully reinforce the theory that no business can operate as an island.

Today's office may be anywhere—and moves from place to place. Wherever you and your work are, that can be your office. Thousands of people work on commuter trains and in planes and find they are especially productive places since they are away from the normal disturbances in the typical office. Some limousines come fully-equipped with the latest business tools, including personal computers, fax machines, and cellular phones.

THE TC

THE TOOLS

The three topics and sections in this chapter are:

Storage

Surfaces

Seating

Buy another wastepaper basket. I know you already have one. But if you invited me to go through that pile of papers on your desk, I could fill both in a trice. To help you decide what to toss and what to save, ask yourself the question asked by the legendary Alfred P. Sloan, Jr.: 'What is the worst that can happen if I throw this out?' If you don't sweat, tremble, or grow faint when you think of the consequences, toss it.

This second wastebasket is a critical investment, even though you'll never be able to fill both on a regular basis. Keep it anyway. It has a symbolic value. It will babysit your in-basket and act like a governess every time you wonder why you bought it.

Ricardo Semler, *Harvard Business Review*, "Managing Without Managers," Sept-Oct 1989

The Paper Clip as Symbol of National Pride:

Norway proudly reminds everyone that the paper clip was invented by Norwegian Johan Vaaler nearly a century ago. The handy little paper holder has also served as a symbol of Norwegian patriotism. During the Nazi occupation, people wore paper clips on their jacket lapels, in silent support of the Jews who were forced to wear the Star of David. The Germans were irritated enough to arrest some people simply for wearing paper clips.

STORAGE

What do office workers need to do their jobs well? That's the key question to ask about tools and it's the one that respon sive and successful furniture manufacturers, space designers, and office managers should all be asking. The question should not have a hypothetical answer; it can most intelligently be an swered by asking the employees themselves, and then folding the individual responses into a larger plan for the office.

We now find storage drawers positioned so they don't bang knees and made of finished materials that don't snag clothes. Lights are everywhere they are needed, not just 12 feet overhead. Surfaces can be adjusted to appropriate heights. Computer screens can swivel. And all this responsiveness yields productivity, not disorganization. Why? Because these choices are made by design—by a guiding idea that says, "This office is built to support the work and workers who make the business happen."

Office tools can be sorted into three broad categories: **storage, surfaces,** and **seating.** Together these three words in clude all office equipment. A paper clip is as rightfully at home in the storage category as a computer is.

OLS

The evolution of tools for the office has followed a process as old as mankind; when a new need arises, somehow—
through trial and error—a tool is shaped to fit the need. Offices,
to a large extent, are concentrations of **communication.**
Most office tools support the need to communicate...a need we
will surely always have with us, which is continually and vigor-
ously supported by the creation, rejection, and adaptation of an
enormous number of tools.

| Paper Original | Carbon Copies | Copier Copies | Electronic Document |

Not long ago there was the original letter, handwritten or
typed, which stood alone as a document. Then came the carbon copy, which enabled you to make two or three duplicates:
one for the boss, one for current files, and possibly one for
long-term records. Photocopying machines revolutionized
matters by making it possible to have unlimited copies. As a

STORAGE

1980	1981	1982	1983	1984	1985	1986	1987	1988	1989	70

mail

60
50
40
30
20

Users in Millions: 10

In the aftermath of the 1989 earthquake in San Francisco, a large architectural firm discovered that only six of its 180 employees were able to function in the building without power. Those who could work were the architects who still drew in pencil on paper and were able to operate in daylight. All the other office employees, being dependent on the telephone, the computer, the CAD machine, the fax machine, and the copier were quite paralyzed.

Ergonomic computing

To evaluate the proper adjustments of your chair and workplace, rest your feet on the floor and adjust your seat until your knees are at approximately a 90 degree angle. Adjust your keyboard height so the home row (asdf, etc.) is equal to your seated elbow height. (This will help you keep your wrists straight.) Sit about three feet from your computer screen and situate it between 10 and 20 degrees below your straight-ahead line of sight…so that you look down at it slightly. Using a polarizing screen and locating light sources so they will not produce glare will reduce eye strain greatly. If you work with a computer all day, take a three-minute break every hour and a 15-minute break every two hours.

result, many more people felt the need to have copies. Being "informed" became an institutionalized ritual, reaching perplexing lengths in the form of "CCs" and "distribution lists."

We live in a time during which the volume of paper being distributed within an average office is expanding faster than the ability to handle it. Contrary to "projections," which clearly were not based on the experience of human nature, **computerization** has not decreased, but rather increased the amount of paper we use. It's estimated that by the year 2000 the ratio of paper storage to electronic storage will be 1:1.

Clearly, paper will be around for a long time. One of the key issues in any office is coping with this paper explosion to reduce the waste, confusion, and anxiety it can cause. Recently a firm of about 100 people recorded that its 8½ x 11" copying paper inventory has increased in five years from 45,000 sheets to 250,000 sheets per month (that's an increase of 556%); in that time, the firm itself had only grown by 50%.

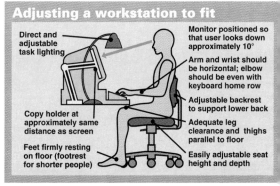

Adjusting a workstation to fit

Direct and adjustable task lighting

Monitor positioned so that user looks down approximately 10°

Arm and wrist should be horizontal; elbow should be even with keyboard home row

Adjustable backrest to support lower back

Copy holder at approximately same distance as screen

Adequate leg clearance and thighs parallel to floor

Feet firmly resting on floor (footrest for shorter people)

Easily adjustable seat height and depth

Storage is really about how you manage information. What's the most important function of storage? **Retrieval.** Buried deep in our genetic code is the message "don't throw that away, you might need it someday." And our genes are right—we need access to a lot of information, but most of it must be stored somewhere at any given moment. If everything was simultaneously on the surface, we'd be completely overwhelmed.

There are hundreds of options available for storage, but before buying a cabinet or designing a fileroom, you should study the storage/retrieval needs of your business. An understanding of the way people organize and **access** information is crucial to the success of any storage plan, and any storage plan must take into account the different definitions of storage.

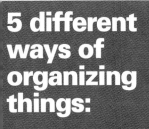

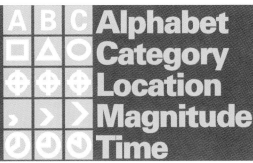

5 different ways of organizing things:

A	B	C	**Alphabet**
□	△	○	**Category**
⊕	⊕	⊕	**Location**
'	>	>	**Magnitude**
◔	◑	◕	**Time**

Offices, like individuals, have a conscious level, a short-term memory, and a long-term memory.

The ways of **organizing information** are finite. Information can be organized by **category** (the name of a project or client), by **time** (chronological files), by **location** (Region 2 Sales, Headquarters, Satellite Offices), by **alphabet** (the method we're most familiar with, but that has no other inherent value), and by **continuum** (smallest to largest, least important to most important, etc.). These modes are applicable to almost any endeavor—from your personal file cabinets to multinational corporations. They are the **framework** upon which annual reports, conversations, exhibitions, directories, conventions, and even warehouses are arranged.

Analyze the uses to which these organizational "hatracks" could be put. It may be that organizing by a continuum of personal relevance instead of by alphabet will result in the destruction, or at least the deep storage, of a great deal of clutter. Similarly, research the different needs people have for information. If they *do* all need access to the same files at different times, then **centralized storage** is probably appropriate. If the operation works better in discrete units, or if security and privacy are paramount needs, then maybe information should be stored by location or work group.

The Rolodex, invented in 1950 and called the "wheel of fortune," is the symbol of the power-driven. Today's Rolodex safeguards the office, home, and car-phone numbers of the rich and famous, a physical testimony to the slogan "It's not what you know, but who you know that counts."

Personal Baggage

Offices need to provide places to hold personal items, too. They need coatracks, closets, drawers, refrigerators. People bring more and more of their home lives into the office; and even if they don't literally "personalize" their space, the amount of time spent in the space makes it personal by default. When an employee makes a commitment to work late or eat lunch at his/her desk (another use for this multifaceted office tool), or

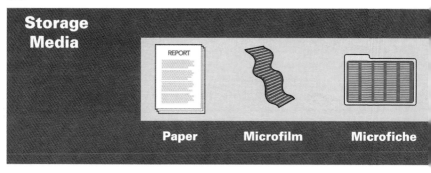

Storage Media

Paper   Microfilm   Microfiche

cancels a personal appointment to meet a professional one, the office can facilitate and support their **dedication.** It can provide some place to store and cook a meal, a private corner for a phone call, somewhere to hang a change of clothes.

Recycling

Recycling is another way of managing the use of paper. It won't be difficult to persuade today's office workers, who are extremely **environmentally aware,** to maintain a paper recycling system. As much as 85% of office waste is discarded paper, and more than 4 million tons of office wastepaper is disposed of each year. According to the American Paper Institute, about 19 million tons of wastepaper is now being reprocessed each year into paper products such as cardboard boxes, newspapers, and more office paper. Today, up to 30% of paper produced comes from recycled paper.

Since recycling has become a profitable business, finding a recycling firm to serve an office is as simple as reading through the Yellow Pages. Costs are controlled; waste is reduced; and the office scores points for its sense of ecologic responsibility.

Filing Options

Half-height drawers
Letter and legal width drawers
Lockable drawers
Hanging files (inside)
Rolling file carts
Rolling file cabinets

Posting shelf
Legal and letter size vertical file
Work shelf
Flat files
Card and coin trays
Wide file drawers

Storage Systems

So it's clear that in designing a storage system for an office, a review of needs must take place first. Once the needs have been identified, meeting them is a matter of becoming familiar with the **options** offered by manufacturers. Needs do not have to be limited to an assumption of what is and is not available; manufacturers have products to meet nearly every storage need imaginable and the industry is by no means sitting still.

| Slides | Electronic Media | Trash Can | File Cabinets |

Many filing systems are now part and parcel of the work surface. Office workers are no longer forced to adapt their work patterns and storage needs to the forced limitation of one pencil drawer and two deep drawers. Storage units these days are *mobile.* They clip on and off, wheel under desks, stack on top of one another. The question these days is getting a hold on what goes into storage, not the options for storage itself.

As it has in other areas, electronics has blurred the distinction between storage and surfaces. It used to be pretty clear that you did your work on a desk and stored that work in a drawer or file cabinet. Now the great percentage of us do at least some of our work on a computer monitor that is parked on a desk only because the desk was already there. When we've completed the task on the screen, we can copy it, print it, store it, or build on it almost simultaneously. The computer is, in essence, our short-term work-memory. Everything we work on can be easily resumed.

Mailrooms

Electronic communication is making inroads on mail service by decreasing the need for letters, stamps, envelopes, even mailrooms. But most companies still rely a lot on "paper" mail. A well-functioning mailroom is important in order to process mail quickly and efficiently. It's the generator that "makes" business happen. Often, though, this room is located in a pokey interior space or dark basement. Lighting is stark; the room cramped and crowded. The design of these places isn't usually treated with the same attention as the design of the rest of the office. Yet it's probably the most important storage area for an office. Realistically, most offices could quite easily exist without many of their managers and other senior personnel; few offices can operate for more than a few days without their mail services. The same concerns about proximity and privacy, efficient storage, ample work surfaces, and comfortable lighting are required in this vital area. Is the mailroom in your office easily accessible to messengers? To express-mail carriers? Near access to trucks? Look into it.

Electronic Storage

One area of storage where you might find expert help useful is in the realm of electronic storage.

At the basic user level, any work done on a computer should be backed up. After that, things can get complicated. Do you need an off-site electronic **archive** so your own system

Too much information for your screen? Xerox Corporation is developing new technology to allow information to be displayed spatially; the user can zoom in for a closer look. Already in use at Xerox's Palo Alto Research Center is an organizational chart that displays the entire management tree, with the names of the people who report to the managers contained in a carousel that whirls out like a Rolodex to display individual names. Rotate for perspective to get a visual of "the big picture." The complexity of the programs that create 3-D displays now requires an expensive workstation to run, but within five years, 3-D imaging should be available on your local desktop.

The latest in computer-structuring technology imitates corporate organizations. The hierarchical "mainframe on top and PC on bottom" is "flattening" into networked PCs that connect to specialty servers with high-powered microprocessor chips for handling calculating, printing, communications, or data-base functions. As corporations have been finding greater speed and maneuverability with entrepreneurial teams of employees, so too the new computer networks with servers both work faster and adapt easily, and inexpensively, to changes.

Local Area Networks
Different Local Area Networks (LANs)

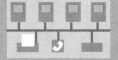

Bus
Computers and peripherals connected in office by spine.

Token Ring
Equipment chained one after another.

Star
Equipment connected to central unit.

Less Is More

When setting up open-plan workstations using panels, there are three things to think about with wiring:

Interface—Where the panel's electrical system hooks up with the building's power source.

Distribution—The path the electricity takes from the power source, through the panel components, to the outlet.

Access—Where the outlet is placed to make it convenient to plug things in.

Electronic Media Options

	Diskette	High Density Diskette	Cartridge	Optical Disk
Size	3.5" x 3.5"	3.5" x 3.5"	5.25" x 5.25"	5.25" x 5.25"
Cap. (MB)	~.8 MB (low)	~1.4 MB (low)	~88 MB (med)	~650 MB (high)
Cap. (text)	~1600 pages	~2800 pages	~176,000 pages	~1,300,000 pages
Price	~$2.50/MB (high)	~$4.50/MB (high)	~90¢/MB (med)	~39¢/MB (low)
Speed	slow	slow	medium	slow
Pros	portable, simple	portable, simple	portable	portable
Cons	magnetic vulner.	magnetic vulner.	magnetic vulner.	stable

	CD-Rom	Video Disk	Hard Drive	Server
Size	4.75" x 4.75"	12" x 12"	10" x 3" x 10"	12" x 9" x 18"
Cap. (MB)	~650 MB (high)	~25,000 MB (very high)	80-600 MB (med)	80-600 MB (med)
Cap. (text)	~1,300,000 pages	NA	170,000-1M pages	170,000-1M pages
Price	~2¢/MB (very low)	~$4.50/MB (high)	~$4-$1.50/MB (high)	~$50-$10/MB (high)
Speed	very slow	very slow	fast	fast
Pros	portable, multimedia	portable, multimedia	portable	multi-user
Cons	stable, read-only	stable, read-only, analog (not digital)	magnetic vulner., not very portable	magnetic vulner., not very portable

doesn't get weighed down? Is your business literally the data-storage business? (It is if you're a publisher, a newspaper, or a research institute.) If so, you need a hyper-efficient data base whose information can be accessed through a number of approaches. Maybe your business is biotechnology or imports/exports. If you keep track of tens of thousands of records then you might need optical storage. Conversely, a three-person office specializing in hand-lettered signs will have much more modest electronic needs.

What the tiny silicon chip did for computers, fiber optic cable has done for telephone and other communications wires.

According to Nicholas Negroponte, the founder and director of MIT's Media Lab, the telephone and television will eventually cross paths as the phone system switches to broadcast transmissions like cellular technology and televisions rely almost exclusively on cable and other "physical" connections.

"Products and Services for Computer Networks," *Scientific American,* September 1991

Electronic Archives

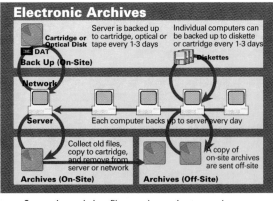

Converting existing files to electronic storage is an expensive process; sometimes it's more practical to keep the documents in paper form, but to track them electronically. Other businesses—libraries, research departments, financial institutions—will find electronic conversion is the only **long-term**

can be created to link files and workers in and out of the office.

Wireless
Computers and peripherals connected via infrared links.

BBS
Computer connected to data-base over phone line.

Modems
Computers connected remotely over phone line.

answer to their storage needs. It probably pays to know the legal definitions of storage; if the IRS or Revenue Canada requires retention for a certain number of years, can that need be met electronically or must the "originals" be kept?

Storerooms are People Too

Ironically, as office designers and business managers increase their understanding of the value of human communication, it may be useful to look at people as "storage units." Every business has its **"archivist"**—informal or otherwise. These people are the corporate equivalent of oral historians, and are invaluable at wading through the knowledge, tradition, and behaviors that have shaped a company. If office design is thought of in terms of corporate culture rather than the placement of phones and furniture, then this kind of "storage" need should be recognized. Do people have as easy access to one another as they do to file cabinets?

TO DO:

Find the "archivist" in your company. This is the person that everyone runs to when they can't find something. He or she is invaluable—especially in an emergency.

Desk Accessories

| Pen Cup | Paper Clip Caddy | Post-It® Note Tray | Picture Frame | Calendar |

The writing on the wall

A senior IBMer recently shifted jobs, taking on an important research assignment in another high-technology company. He walked into an executive's office several weeks after arriving, closed the door, and said, "I've got a problem." The executive blanched; the fellow was critical to his plans. "I don't understand why you don't have blackboards around here," said the ex-IBMer. "How do you people talk to each other and exchange ideas without blackboards everywhere?" His point was well taken. Tom Watson, Sr., started the thrust at IBM with his ubiquitous use of butcher paper on a stand. Physical trappings such as these help spur the intense, informal communication that underpins regular innovation.

Tom Peters and Bob Waterman, *In Search of Excellence*

Things to be found in a typical desk:

Paper clips, Push pins,
Paper, Notepads, Post-It® notes,
Paper punch, Stapler, Scissors,
Change of shoes,
Purse/Wallet, Change (money),
Pens, Pencils, Erasers, Markers,
Correction fluid, Diskettes, Keys,
Labels, Business cards, Envelopes,
Letter opener, Staple remover,
Rubber bands, Tape, Glue,
Candy bar, Toothbrush, Toothpaste
Address book, Date books,
Voodoo doll of manager,
Art supplies, Ruler,
File tabs, Napkins, Plastic flatware,
Sugar, Salt, Pepper, Soy sauce packets,
More candy bars

SURFACES

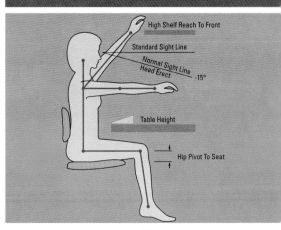

The more encompassing office design becomes, the clearer certain patterns become as well. The most obvious insight that a "whole office" approach offers is a recognition that few components operate independently. Electronics have helped to blur any pre-existing distinctions, but even those were forced. Is a desk a "work surface" or a "storage unit"? Is a wall an "acoustical necessity" or a useful tool for presentations? Is a computer for working faster or is it for working better?

Surfaces are flat, wide open spaces, places that support work and equipment. The most basic surfaces are the desk and the worktable: horizontal surfaces on which to write, read, draw, or undertake a specific task. Surfaces need to be related to business needs and **human dimensions.** Tables and desks are at a certain height above the floor and above a chair because the worker is usually seated. That height has to be related to eye and arm level if writing is involved, or at a level that is comfortable for keyboard use.

For some tasks (such as drawing or sketching), it's helpful to have adjustable surfaces to minimize strain and to maximize individual productivity.

The fundamental consideration in the basic work surface is its relationship to the human being and the tasks that person is performing. Desk and table heights should be at different levels depending on whether the primary tasks are inputting, typing, drafting, or writing. A lot of managers use desks as storage units but don't sit at them much during the day. A secretary or accountant needs a desk that integrates into the job—everything accessible, at comfortable heights—optimizing performance. In

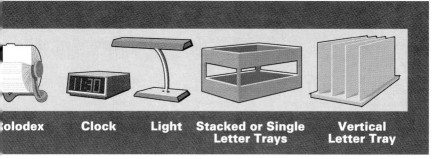

| Rolodex | Clock | Light | Stacked or Single Letter Trays | Vertical Letter Tray |

other words, for many functions, the charm of the rolltop and its myriad cubbyholes is quickly put to test when the desk is put to practical use.

The obvious path into designing with surfaces is to talk about desks. Traditionally, these define position, power, and placement in an office. Each of us has glimpsed a CEO's office and seen the highly polished shine of mahogany. We've all been to the motor vehicle department, where government-issue desks dare you to ask for special treatment.

These days, and for the discernible future, when you think about a **work surface,** you are thinking, at least in part, about a place to rest a personal computer. People need work surfaces (a.k.a. desks or tables) for other reasons, as well—to write notes, to review information, to eat lunch and work at the same time, to collate papers and reports—and, of course, the telephone has to go somewhere. Desks still play an important role in office organization. And even if the use of the surface was not an issue, the arrangement and placement of desks and how that organizes office space remains. This is one of the most tangible and important issues in office design—how do the tools assist in organizing the space for optimal individual and group performance. Decisions about work surfaces should draw on individual needs—but those individual needs will shift and continue to be refined and rethought at a micro level by the individual worker. The office manager/space planner has the task of effectively subordinating personal needs to the composite needs of the larger organization.

The health issues arising with prolonged computer use are both personal and business concerns. If the office is new or still under construction, invest the design with measures that reduce or prevent health problems. **Retrofitting** a traditional office is expensive, but this cost may be inevitable. No business can afford an unnecessary expense; perhaps it's best to view this as long-term savings rather than short-term cost.

Things to remember when planning for workstations in the office

Is the lighting s
to avoid gla⟩

Is distance between opera
and monitor at least 10"-1⟩

What types of software interf⟩
will your workers most easily u⟩

What types of jobs or tasks will
be performed on this machine?

Is the keyboard at typing hei⟩
and at least 15" away from the operat⟩

Furniture Systems

Certainly no design of an office today can ignore what is known generically as **"systems furniture."** Systems are what they sound like: pieces that can be combined and integrate⟩ in a variety of ways depending on the need of the office. The cornerstone of most furniture systems is a **"work surface"** —this equates to the flat horizontal surface of the familiar desk and is available in at least as many sizes and materials as the traditiona⟩ desk. The work surface, however, is adjustable because it either is hung from a framework of panels that also supports drawers, file cabinets, bulletin boards, and more work surfaces, or is part of an easily dismantled and put-back-together unit assembly. Because systems furniture is, at its essence, adaptable, it has not been outmoded by the advent of the electronic office. The panel⟩ that make up the basic system components are also designed to accommodate cable for telephones, lights, and computers.

One obvious merit of designing with systems furniture is the ability to design with **growth** and change in mind. This assumes that office design is itself seen as an essential contributor to that growth. The investment in good systems furniture is one that is often given the third-degree by the "puny payoff" people. The question about systems furniture, or any new technology, product, service, or idea, should not be "can we afford it?" but rather "is it valuable?" If the question centers around value rather than cost, at least the answer (positive or negative) will have responded to the key issue. Panels can do what sheetrock and drywall once did—they're moveable and they become definers of departments or teams. They reduce clutter and increase efficiency by concealing wiring, and at the same time, they bring power to an employee's equipment. And sys-

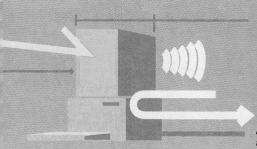

What are the dimensions, cabling connections, and weight?

Is appropriate noise control (doors, walls, enclosures) available?

Are ventilation and temperature adequate?

Are cables and wires away from the floors?

tems furniture is increasingly a pleasure to look at. Personal choice in furnishings and color is not surrendered when one opts for systems furniture. This is part of the process of empowerment we talked about earlier. Manufacturers of systems furniture—the smart ones—are as sensitive as any savvy businessperson is to who really makes a decision. If an office planner, as a customer, cannot find furniture that suits his or her needs and taste, then the manufacturer and the designer who represents that manufacturer will have fallen down on the job, lost a sale, and, more importantly, an opportunity.

Not everyone likes to work at a desk or work surface or even a **workstation.** (In the language of office design, a workstation is a "wholly contained" work environment that includes a personal computer as part of its basic design.) A lot of people prefer to work on tables. There is ease of **movement** and ability to keep many projects going at once. Any person whose job requires frequent meetings should at least have the option of a table—it can strike the right note of formality for signing papers and it can suggest a place where open discussion is encouraged.

Table Talk

Some offices seem wed to the notion of traditional desks, even though their usefulness is long since gone. A law office may want to project an image of centuries-old tradition, but how about a travel agency? A **customer** goes in and sits on a chair facing the travel agent. It's like being called to the principal's office. The customer's knees bang against the desk, and he can't really get at the information the agent is manipulating a mile a minute on a computer. In this atmosphere, customers feel like they're being punished rather than planning a pleasurable vacation. If ever an office cried out for chairs, couches, and low tables where a relaxed, informal conversation could take place, this is it. The computer would be there, of course, but it would be called upon to check facts, not scare travelers out of their options.

Tables are usually found in conference rooms, meeting rooms, and lunchrooms. Most offices accommodate these spaces, formally or informally. A lot of pop psychology goes into the conference table: Where's the power seat? How many people can efficiently conduct business at once? Should the chairs be stiff or comfortable? The most important consideration in designing meeting rooms is to make sure you have enough of them and that they're adaptable for different uses. For every business that can afford the splendid isolation of an execu-

A word about computers

Just when office designers were finally beginning to design around people, along came personal computers, those finicky, delicate machines that we suddenly can't do without. They need to be cooled; they take up desk space we used to use for writing; they need *more* space for their printers (which are often noisy); the lighting needs change because of screen glare; desks need to change because keyboards have to be at the correct heights; we start to get backaches...

But we design around all this because the computer really has become indispensable. Computations and reports can be made in a fraction of the time they used to take, giving companies a more immediate look at the health of their business. Writing can be corrected, edited, and improved much more easily than before. Files can be sent across the country at the speed of light. Corporate communications improve because workers feel more comfortable sending e-mail messages instead of traditional mail to higher-ups. This also conserves paper.

A keyboard-terraced desk is a desk with a lower shelf or moveable arm where a keyboard sits at a lower height than the rest of a computer's components. This allows a user's arms and wrists to be at a better angle for typing. Keyboard-terraced desks can greatly reduce muscle fatigue and may help prevent keyboard-related health problems.

Capacity of CD-ROMs

270,000 sheets of paper
2835 lb

Weight (in lb)
of various storage media
capable of storing
540 MB of data

1500 floppy disks
54.44 lb

1000 microfiches
2.96 lb

1 CD-ROM in a "Jewel Box"
0.21 lb

tive boardroom, there are hundreds more that need space for **team interaction,** employee meetings, and shirtsleeve presentations to clients.

If you think the boardroom is a luxury, you're probably right—but every business needs what used to be called a **"war room."** A more fashionable term these days might be a "solutions room," but the basic idea—strategic planning and teamwork—is unchanged. The disappearance of the private office makes these "alternative" spaces a necessity. Make sure the room is soundproofed, well-ventilated, and well-lit. Tables and chairs should fit comfortably in the room and the furniture should speak convincingly for the business.

Walls are an essential component of office design—and not merely because they hold the place up and keep Accounting from seeping into Sales. In creative businesses (design studios, architectural firms, advertising agencies), the project pin-up is part of the designer's job. The designer's ideas go up on the wall for all to see. He or she is expected to use the wall to orga-

nize ideas and explain concepts. Any meeting room can accommodate push pins or likely substitutes such as charts, white boards (some of which can produce their own photocopies), or even chalkboards. Wall presentations invite **collaboration** and **interaction.** When the great American architect Louis Kahn designed the Salk Institute at La Jolla, California, he stipulated that chalkboards be placed strategically in the open public circulation areas between the laboratories and the private of-

fices. Then scientists could use them for informal discussions and demonstrations outside their labs. At the workstation level, people need tack boards. Not everything can be filed or set on a desk—sometimes information is just urgent enough that it should hang at eye level. Schedules, timelines, and to-do lists often make their way to walls and bulletin boards.

If the entire office is envisioned as a workable surface, office design can be that much more creative and participative. Regardless of the price of office space, efficient use of rentable space should be maximized. So, while planning space around systems furniture, sufficient power outlets, and so on—the plan should expand to other spaces and how they can be adapted to practical use. The fact is, people use the floor around their desks. No amount of desk surface or storage will do when you need to collate 20 copies of a 50-page document, review files before an audit, or shift file systems.

Office Chairs Through History

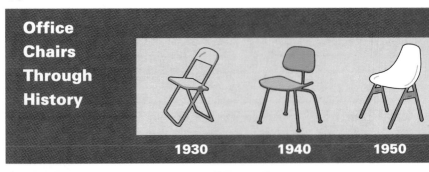

1930   **1940**   **1950**

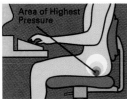

Taking good care of your ischial tuberosities

Ischial tuberosities isn't the name for a lung disease or an exotic type of vegetable.

Ischial tuberosities are the two small "sitting bones" in the buttocks. Pressure on these bones over a long period of time becomes extremely uncomfortable. Good chairs help distribute and cushion the body's weight to prevent too much pressure on these sensitive areas.

To rule is not so much a question of the heavy hand as the firm seat.

Ortega y Gasset

"...a skyscraper seemed almost easier to design than a chair."

Mies van der Rohe

"...all my life my legs have been banged up somewhere by the chairs I designed."

Frank Lloyd Wright

SEATING

The Office Chair
Instrument of torture or ergonomic delight?

In the last 30 years, great strides have been made in developing chairs that are designed for comfort and efficiency. Traditionally, people who are required to spend the most time in chairs (typists, data-entry operators, and other clerical workers) have been given the most uncomfortable chairs. After receiving a complaint that workers tipped over backwards trying to "adjust" his chairs, Frank Lloyd Wright is said to have responded, "Well, they won't do it twice, will they?"

The **task chair** as we know it dates back to when typewriters were introduced into the office. The first task chair, known as the secretarial chair, was armless, mounted on wheels, and featured a low, adjustable back. Clerical workers who sat at typewriters, adding machines, or switchboards all day got these small, "functional" (uncomfortable) chairs, while

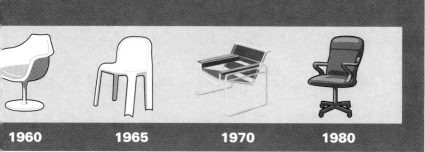

| 1960 | 1965 | 1970 | 1980 |

heir bosses got the leather-upholstered thrones (equally nfunctional and uncomfortable, but at least impressive). **Functionality,** of course, was decided by the owner or the designer, not by the user and the task. The three-wheeled chairs designed for the Johnson Wax building reflected Frank Lloyd Wright's (and, in general, all designers') total indifference to worker comfort. In the '20s and '30s, chairs were designed mainly for style, influenced by Bauhaus design, with spare tubular steel components. Things improved with Charles Eames' molded plywood and fiberglass chairs, which were contoured to the body. In 1965 Charles Pollack's classic swivel armchair signified a recognition of the relationship between comfort and performance.

Sitting for long periods of time in a bad chair is like sleeping in a bad mattress. The result is health problems, especially **backaches.** Backaches, or any other illness, translate into lost productivity and absenteeism. An illness that relates to the performance of a tool can probably be remedied by fixing (or replacing) the tool. In fact, backaches and legs going to sleep can be a direct result of sitting in a poorly designed chair. Chairs designed for the "average" person don't really work. Since nobody is exactly average, the chairs don't fit anyone. A good chair allows the user to adjust not only the height, but also the tension of the backrest and the position of the legs. A chair seat should have a rounded front edge to prevent cutting off leg circulation. A well-performing chair will support its users for long periods of sitting without causing discomfort.

This brings us to **ergonomics,** which is best described as the study of matching the environment, tools, and work process to the needs of workers and the organization. Simply, it's about making the "best fit" between people and environment. Most businesses today realize how important a comfortable workplace is. And comfortable doesn't mean lounge chairs and footrests. What an effective office design needs is seating that contributes to employee job satisfaction and performance and prevents employee disability.

The Diffrient Executive Chair (1978), hailed as a great advance in ergonomics, swiveled and tilted and could support a reclining person. For several years after its introduction, a simple swivel-and-tilt chair was considered the answer to the problem of comfort in the office. But when people tilted back in these chairs, their necks stiffened and their feet often lifted off the floor, which tended to cut off circulation to the lower legs and feet. This led to the invention of the knee-tilt mechanism, which enables people to lean back while keeping their feet on the floor.

10 features to look for in a good office chair:

1. A chair back that supports but also allows free movement

2. Downward curving [or short] armrests so the chair can pull close to work surfaces

3. Lumbar support for the lower back to prevent fatigue

4. Backrest and seat that move independently

5. Upholstery that's stain- and fire-resistant

6. Lumbar support for the legs that also allows for easy movement (free blood circulation to the feet and lower legs)

7. Adjustable knee-tilt mechanisms that permit adjusting for the comfort of the lower legs and feet

8. Adjustable tilt tension

9. Adjustable seat height (either pneumatic or mechanical)

10. A space-saving base that also provides stability to the chair

Progressive Architecture,
"The Ultimate Office Chair,"
May 1988

Chair parts

Armrests are optional and may or may not be covered in the same material as seat

Headrest (optional) should be available if chair reclines

Backrest should be height-adjustable

Seat pan height should be adjustable

Armrest (optional)

Strut may be fixed, or include a pneumatic or mechanical height adjustment

Base may have casters, glides (non-rolling), or a sled base

Adding adjustments and knobs and levers to chairs initially created more problems. Since the mechanisms were not usually explained to the users, the employees could not or would not adjust their chairs, and many were more uncomfortable than if they'd been sitting in a simple straight-back chair. Now chairs are becoming simpler and easier to operate. Finally (and not a moment too soon) a **"thinking" ergonomic chair** has been created that requires little active participation on the part of the user. These pliant chairs adjust automatically to the routine bends and turns a person makes while working.

Choosing office chairs today involves more than picking the style and color (although, fortunately, your options in those areas include a wide range of colors, fabrics, and styles). Learning from past example, it makes sense to fully understand the *range* of work performed in the office and then make chair selections accordingly. As with fancy stereo systems, there's no sense buying furniture that's "loaded" beyond your needs; the opposite, of course, is true, too—even when working at home, a dining-room chair will not serve you well as a computer-table chair over the long haul.

The key thing to consider is a chair's ability to support the work done by the person sitting in it. Whatever the chair costs, if it isn't designed to fit and move with the human form, it's a waste of money. Chair comfort (and other environmental comforts) affects **environmental satisfaction** for all types

Adjusting A Chair To Fit

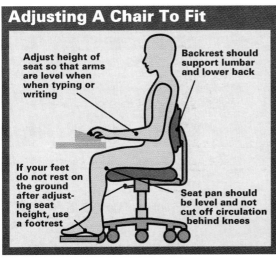

Adjust height of seat so that arms are level when when typing or writing

Backrest should support lumbar and lower back

If your feet do not rest on the ground after adjusting seat height, use a footrest

Seat pan should be level and not cut off circulation behind knees

of jobs and is a strong determinant of overall comfort in the office. While comfort is determined by several factors in the workplace—amount of space, degree of enclosure, temperature fluctuation, noises from talking and equipment, overall illumination, computer glare, and so on—the chair is probably *the* most immediate piece of equipment affecting worker performance and workplace satisfaction. Remember, a worker spends three-quarters of the day in one.

The challenge is for business owners to provide comfortable and efficient equipment for their employees without straining their budget. Is this possible? Manufacturers, aware of the importance of supportive equipment to their bottom line (so to speak) are continually investing in research and design to come up with furniture that suits the needs of the human body and the demands of technology. When all else fails, ask.... If a need you have isn't being met, it should be.

The large executive chair elevates the sitter. It distances him. It protects the body. There is a tall back to rest [his head] and it is covered with the skin of some animal, preferably your predecessor.

Emilio Ambasz, New York architect and industrial designer

Test Driving an Office Chair

Choosing the right office chair is no easy matter—the quality of your choice affects worker comfort, health, and on-the-job performance. Sit in a chair before you buy it, and make sure it does the following:

1. Provides support for the lower back

2. Has a seat that isn't too deep (watch out for this—seats that tip up in front cut off circulation to the legs)

3. Doesn't allow you to ever feel the hard inner shell of the chair while seated. Don't be fooled by how "cushy" a chair looks—the best manufacturers often use a thin cushion and still pass this test easily

4. Has arms, casters, cushions, and other parts that are easily maintained or replaced in your office

5. Meets or exceeds the standards for seating dimensions and adjustability established by the American National Standards Institute/Human Factors Society

6. Pleases the eye

THE PL

The three topics and sections in this chapter are:

Sight

Light

Sound

Eighty percent of success is showing up.

Woody Allen

Barrier-Free Design

Having your workplace accessible to disabled employees and visitors is smart business and, in most places now, legally required. Some things to consider in designing a barrier-free office:

fire-safe stairwells

access ramps

extra-wide corridors and doorways to accommodate wheelchairs

wheelchair access for telephones, wall light switches, and electrical outlets

braille markings on signage and in elevators for the visually impaired

strobe fire alarms for the hearing impaired

accessible vending machines should have coin inserts at a height within reach of someone in a wheelchair

Can a well-designed office improve productivity? Nearly seven in 10 of today's office workers think so. But an office is a bundle of conflicting requirements. This is an important point. Available space and budget have to accommodate optimal efficiency *and* human factors.

So much of designing for the environment involves very **subjective issues.** Color, light, and comfort are individual preferences. Personal tastes and varied office duties make each person's needs different. Do any two people agree on which color is most pleasing and how much light is enough to see their tasks? Will an employee from Hawaii be happy with an office temperature pleasing to someone from Maine? Can one worker keep going if a freight train goes by, while another is distracted by the sound of staplers? Should a manager care? Employees who complain about how cold it is or can't see the computer screen without squinting are employees who are distracted from their work. **Comfort** yields productivity.

There is also a psychological aspect to listening to employee needs. When management tells employees that they are

CE

It is true that some plants actually help clean the air by removing pollutants. Some plants can de-pollute the air for up to 100 square feet. The plants that work best include: golden pothos, spider plants, philodendron, bamboo palm, gerbera daisy, peace lily, chrysanthemum, warneckie, and corn plants. These are effective at eliminating formaldehydes, smoke, trichloroeth-ylene, benzene, and gases emitted from plastics and oils.

being empowered to take control of their work in order to do the best job they can, employees are engaged and can focus more on the needs at hand. Employees who can't control their work environment are dissatisfied and less productive employ-ees. Having to go through a manager and the facilities depart-ment (and still not getting a decent room temperature) is a frus-trating waste of time. Where possible, controls that allow employees to adjust temperature, sound masking, and lighting in their own areas provide a tremendous morale boost and alleviate **environmental distractions.**

When setting up an office, observe the basic standards that dictate what humans consider a physically comfortable climate. Then let the people who work there decide. If seven or eight out of 10 employees agree, then consider it comfortable. The others can use sweaters, small fans, task lights, sound barriers, or what-ever it takes to make their environment usable.

Place issues go beyond mere aesthetics to concerns for safety and health. You may remember or have read about the outbreak of Legionnaire's Disease in May 1976. The press

How to get a landlord to change HVAC settings...

1. Offer to do it yourself; this alone brings them running.

2. Call as often as you need to and articulate your concerns in terms of the impact they're having on your business.

3. Ask what steps you can take "locally" to minimize discomfort.

4. Do not settle for the answer "We have to take the whole building into account." Your needs are legitimate.

5. Be realistic. The HVAC for an open plan will be different than that for enclosed offices; an older building's system will differ from that in the newly constructed building.

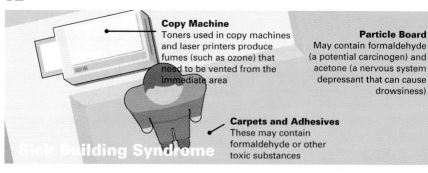

Copy Machine
Toners used in copy machines and laser printers produce fumes (such as ozone) that need to be vented from the immediate area

Particle Board
May contain formaldehyde (a potential carcinogen) and acetone (a nervous system depressant that can cause drowsiness)

Carpets and Adhesives
These may contain formaldehyde or other toxic substances

Sick Building Syndrome

SBS: What to do

1. Be aware:
Education is the first step to curing a sick office. Ask the right questions. What is in the products you use? What are things made of? Are they harmful to us?

2. Source removal:
Remove hazardous products like vinyl asbestos tiles, lead-infested oil-base paint, etc.

3. Source isolation:
Isolate the toxic product away from people and habitable spaces. An emergency generator, for instance, runs on noxious diesel fuel. Don't put it in near the air-conditioning ducts. The same is true for a smoking room. Keep cigarette smoke away from the air-conditioning system so smoke doesn't circulate throughout the office.

4. Source substitution:
Substitute non off-gassing products. Use vinyl composition tiles instead of vinyl asbestos, etc.

5. Ventilation dilution:
Allow air to circulate and bring in clean outside air to dilute contaminated indoor air. Don't put the intake duct next to the exhaust.

Anthony Bernheim, AIA

Harvard Business Review

"Miss Osener, this office needs brightening up. See if you can find something with a summer view, looking across a body of water, maybe a bay with a village clinging to steep hills in the distance, trees, mountains, sailboats…kind of Mediterranean by someone fairly well known, preferably French and not over five million."

described it as the "greatest medical mystery of the century" (this was before AIDS). People throughout the world were shocked when an unidentifiable illness infected 221 and killed 34 American Legion members at their state convention in Philadelphia. Its cause was finally traced to an organism that was transmitted through the air-conditioning system of the Bellevue-Stratford Hotel, headquarters of the convention. This incident made people aware for the first time that indoor air could be contaminated and, as in this case, more harmful than outdoor air.

In the last 20 years, office workers have moved into sealed buildings whose environments are almost completely regulated by technology. In these smart buildings, people risk their health every day by being exposed to toxins in recycled air, lack of natural light and fresh air, and the mental and physical stress of using computers all day long. Maladies such as "Sick Building Syndrome" were not really identified until 1980, but now more than half of office workers complain of it. Sick Building Syndrome (SBS) is a factor in falling productivity and rising absenteeism among office workers.

What is SBS? It's a group of symptoms that can't be readily pinned to any particular cause. These symptoms include: headaches, nausea, eye irritations, stuffy nose, dry throat, rashes, and lethargy. An office is considered "sick" if more than 20% of its occupants experience any of these symptoms at work. Although the symptoms are nonspecific, most of them are caused by bacteria or toxins that circulate in the air.

SBS isn't a problem we can ignore or brush off as employee hypochondria. It's having a big impact on businesses,

Air Vents
Vents may draw in fumes from automobile exhaust, roofing materials, or air pollution from the outside. Also, toxins, viruses, smoke, and dust from inside may be recirculated. Air-conditioning system may generate and circulate carbon monoxide

Latex Caulking Around Windows
May contain benzene (a known carcinogen and central nervous system depressant), which may cause irritation

Fluorescent Lights
Flicker may cause distractions and headaches if too frequent

Cigarette Smoke
Well-ventilated areas must be set aside for smoking or smoking should be banned completely inside the building

costing millions of dollars in workers compensation, litigation, and reduced productivity. Much research and attention has been focused on **indoor-air quality.** According to The National Institute of Occupational Safety and Health (NIOSH), which studied 700 buildings, 50% of all indoor-air problems occur in the offices' ventilation systems. Indoor-air quality is one of the biggest issues in office design.

Another pressing environmental concern is the health effects computers are having on the tens of millions of people working with them every day. We don't yet know all the risks. The latest research evidence shows that exposure to **very low frequency radiation** (VLF) does not increase the risk of getting cancer or incurring pregnancy problems.

A study released by NIOSH reported that 40% of 834 reporters and other employees at *Newsday* in New York showed symptoms of repetitive strain injuries—disabling injuries to the hand, wrist, arms, and lower back stemming from the cumulative effects of repeatedly performing a job in an awkward position for extended periods of time. RSIs are being reported in almost every industry, from meat-packing to data processing. They account for almost half of the workplace illnesses reported by the US government.

Very Low Frequency (VLF) Radiation

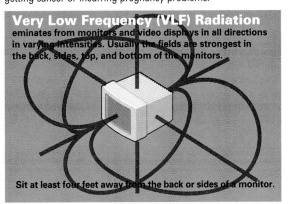

eminates from monitors and video displays in all directions in varying intensities. Usually the fields are strongest in the back, sides, top, and bottom of the monitors.

Sit at least four feet away from the back or sides of a monitor.

One proven danger is that people who make rapid keystrokes all day long are more likely to develop a debilitating illness such as **carpal tunnel syndrome** (CTS), a repetitive strain injury that can cripple the hands. Medical treatment is expensive and often ineffective. After back pain, CTS is one of the most common worker injuries reported today, running up staggering costs in workers compensation, absenteeism, and medical fees.

San Francisco recently passed landmark legislation to prevent "electronic sweatshops" from taking a health toll on workers, but some businesses fought the law, claiming that costs for implementing the guidelines were too high. The courts, in fact, subsequently overturned the legislation on the grounds that only the state has the authority to regulate safety and health issues. Nonetheless, many companies went ahead and made the improvements, knowing that improved employee attendance, health, and morale will more than make up the cost of the investment.

what hazards do you perceive in your office?

Office Workers

47%	Eyestrain
37%	Quality of Air
36%	Radiation from VDTs
33%	Repetitive Strain Injuries
19%	Hazardous Materials

Top Executives

36%	Eyestrain
25%	Quality of Air
24%	Radiation from VDTs
28%	Repetitive Strain Injuries
12%	Hazardous Materials

OEI Survey 1991

Carpal Tunnel Syndrome is an increasingly common repetitive strain injury (RSI) resulting from repetitious hand and wrist movements. The tendons and median nerve pass through the carpal tunnel, a bony structure in the wrist. With continual flexing of the fingers and wrist, the tendon sheaths swell or the bent wrist compresses the nerve. This leads to numbness, tingling, or burning sensations in the palms, fingers, and wrists. Because these symptoms usually occur after the day's work is done, they often go unrecognized as being serious or connected with working conditions. In advanced stages, CTS may require surgery.

Carpal Tunnel Syndrome

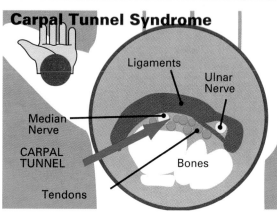

Most offices are in leased or rented spaces, so many business owners or managers don't have full control over the workplace. In many offices, the employees have to call the building manager when the office is too hot and then wait for a technician to temporarily solve the problem. When designing an office, be aware of the factors that can add to or detract from environmental comfort and health. Where you do have control, encourage design solutions that meet the employees' needs. And be informed on the issues when you meet with the building management about areas in which they have control.

Bursa shoulder is a repetitive strain injury caused by continuous work at a video display terminal, drawing board, or other workstation that requires a great deal of arm movement. It is a serious injury that can cause permanent damage if not treated and can be avoided by taking frequent breaks to relieve muscle strain.

Bursa Shoulder

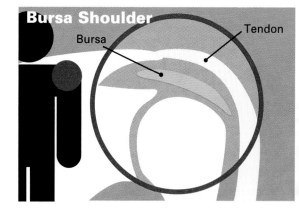

SIGHT

What can you see from where you sit? Does what you see make you feel better about where you are and what you're doing?

People work best when they can **focus** on their immediate tasks and avoid distractions. The private office with its outside window gives the occupant an environment that is both private and connected to the outside world. The walls can be used for furnishings or display. The window offers refreshing views. It orients the gazer to the time of day and the weather, refreshes strained eyes, connects with the rest of the world and with one's personal outside-work life. A window that opens is a bonus, but it's becoming a relic.

If you work in a computerized environment, however, a window is a mixed blessing. If your computer is located near a window, you can get **glare** on the screen and strain your eyes. The modern workstation is designed to achieve all the qualities of the private office and to offer some improvements. The panels surrounding the desk give both privacy and visual relief. Their surfaces provide places for display and storage, as well as protection from unwanted sound. Additionally, the layout of the workstation should allow for long-distance views, so its inhabitant can see the outside or other workers within the group or department.

The eyes of today's workers bounce from dark surfaces to light, from screen to paper. When working on both a writing surface and a computer screen, the eyes are strained by continual adjustment. On a typical video display terminal, the type is light against a black background. If the office worker is looking from screen to written text sitting on a desk, it's a good idea to avoid a dark color for the desk surface so the eyes aren't strained by the contrast between surfaces. Also, matte surfaces produce less glare than shiny ones.

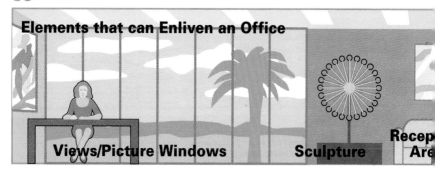

Elements that can Enliven an Office

Views/Picture Windows   Sculpture   Recep
Are

The Office Headache

Conventional strip lighting in offices and flickering computer screens may cause headaches and eyestrain at least once a week for one in 10 office workers, according to British psychologist Dr. Arnold Wilkins.

The rate of flicker in normal fluorescent tubes—100 pulses a second—cannot be seen but affects nerve cells in the eye and brain. These can cause headaches and in some people can speed up the heart rate, perhaps triggering a panic attack for agoraphobics.

New high-frequency lighting tubes exist that pulse too rapidly to affect the brain. These are twice as expensive as conventional lighting tubes, but could reduce absenteeism and the lower productivity that results from fatigue and headaches.

Dr. Wilkins also reported that computer screens can cause tired eyes, as the flicker from screens makes reading more difficult than from printed paper. It's possible that the next generation of computers, which uses liquid crystals rather than cathode ray tubes, will reduce this problem.

Manchester Guardian Weekly,
2 September 1990

We need different sight stimuli to remain active and alert. The eye muscles require a variety of focusing to stay healthy. A worker who stares at a VDT all day needs to take frequent eye breaks. A view through a window to a picture on the wall or to a row of indoor plants is not just an "extra," it serves an important function. NASA research on claustrophobia found that one way to counteract the feeling of confinement was to provide pictures that have a lot of visual depth. Astronauts could psychologically break out of their confined space by "losing themselves" in the pictures. Maybe this is applicable to the intensive VDT user.

Sight goes both ways. What do people see from the moment they arrive at the front door to your office? The sign on the door? Is there a logo? Is the sign a bold display of super graphics or small and discreet? Is it etched in brass? Upon entering the reception area, what's the first thing they see? An original Monet? For some, it pays to spend millions not only for investment purposes, but as an impressive presentation to the public that says this company is a patron and connoisseur of great art—the implication being that the company is equally astute and discerning in business (and successful enough to shell out millions of dollars for a bit of wall decor).

Like fashion for an individual, an office's "look" or design tells a powerful story about that business and how it presents itself to the world. A doctor's office is expected to look clean; the staff wears white coats to reassure patients and convey an air of expertise. A law firm may establish its erudite, traditional image in fine materials, leather, wool carpets, and walls lined with books. An advertising agency wants to communicate its flair and energy in contemporary, innovative design. Office design works as a power tool. It can get first meetings off to a good start. Artwork, decorative details, and personal memen-

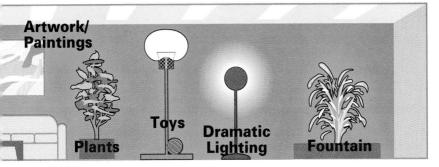

Artwork/ Paintings

Plants

Toys

Dramatic Lighting

Fountain

Decorating the office

You don't have to be like the investor who paid $53.9 million for a Van Gogh to spruce up his office. But artwork helps to humanize workplaces. It softens a high-tech environment. Art serves many functions: It sparks thought, boosts morale, fuels the company image, and gives strained eyes a rest. Whether you opt for an original oil painting, a fine quality reproduction, a limited edition print, or an inexpensive poster (matted and framed), remember that its subliminal message projects the company's image. If you want a positive image, make sure you can afford the art!

tos create opportunities for communication. The reception area stirs interest; design and artistic elements such as sculpture, paintings, colorful furnishings, and photographs are things to talk about that can break the ice and inspire confidence and enthusiasm.

Color

There's one element about sight that touches every part of the office and everyone who works there: Color. Walls, ceilings, floors, and furniture all have to have colors chosen for them, and the choices will affect everyone in the office. Artists, poets, and interior designers have long known about color's persuasive and revealing qualities. Color decisions can't be taken lightly.

In many offices, employees who complain to the facilities manager of being too cold all the time stop complaining when the office is painted a "warmer" color. Passengers on one airline complained of nausea until the plane interiors were repainted—they had been green. Fast-food restaurants are

Are your lobby sofas covered in turquoise and orange vinyl? You got them in the early '60s, right? Paint, carpet, and furniture colors move in and out of fashion the same way clothing colors do, but on a much slower timeline. Even so, a good chair or panel should outlast a color phase, and should be easy to re-upholster. Even basic schemes change: '70s browns gave way to greys in the '80s, but beige is working its way back in for the '90s. So too are the other earth tones of the late '60s—fashion experts call it the "return to earth." More subtle than the previous earthy palette, colors draw inspiration from minerals, metals, and nature.

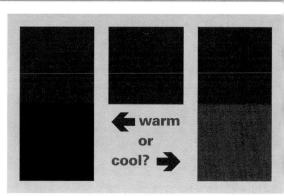

warm
or
cool?

You've probably heard the terms "warm" and "cool" applied to colors. Unfortunately, it isn't as easy as "fire" colors and "ice" colors. Warm means a color tends toward a yellow or orange hue. Cool means that it tends toward a blue or purple hue. But beware; these attributes are all relative. Any color is warmer than some and cooler than others. A fiery red is warmer than blue but still cooler than orange.

To further compound the confusion, warm or cool lighting affects the sharpness of detail. Warm light tends to be sharper and stronger (like the noonday sun). Cool light tends to be softer and fuzzier, with less contrast.

designed with yellow and orange because those colors supposedly stimulate the appetite, and a rapid turnover. Worker productivity improved and absenteeism dropped when a certain factory's dark walls were repainted a lighter color—the "closing in" feeling had lessened.

Although color is very much a matter of **personal taste,** some general features hold true for most people. Yellows, oranges, and reds are called **"warm"** colors, and they can have a stimulating effect on people whose jobs require boring and repetitive tasks. Blues, greens, and purples are **"cool"** colors that can provide a calm and restful atmosphere for writers and designers, but may be depressing for others. Dark colors—especially black—can create either a claustrophobic or a sophisticated atmosphere, depending on how they are treated. Light colors—including white—can look airy, cheerful, and bright, or simply glaring. Color will also be affected by the type of light that illuminates the colored surface.

You normally think about putting color and texture on furniture, walls, ceilings, and floors. But other surfaces, such as panels, screens, desks, and storage units, can be decorated, too. File cabinets come in different colors of "texturized" paint that help to reduce glare from overhead lights and slightly soften the metal surface.

Up to about 10 years ago, panels and walls were treated, as designers say, "tactically." That meant fabrics and paint were applied to disguise manufacturing blips or to cover up wiring, nails, and other signs of construction or imperfection. Now designers use upholstery and color "strategically" to create moods and manipulate the "atmosphere" in a place. Color can help establish architectural elements such as conference rooms or private offices, and designate particular departments.

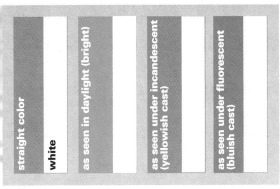

straight color	white	as seen in daylight (bright)	as seen under incandescent (yellowish cast)	as seen under fluorescent (bluish cast)

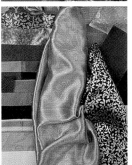

Before you choose colors and fabrics, determine your company image: Is it fashion-conscious? Do the latest color or design fads have an impact on your business? They do for many design, architecture, advertising, and fashion-related organizations. This may involve redecorating every two or three years or so. Are you planning a thorough redecoration? Or can you get away with re-doing the reception room? You can choose a palette for a longer duration, something that will last beyond short-term crazes. The middle-of-the-road solution to office aesthetics is to sift out the fads from the trends.

If you're completely redecorating or starting from scratch, then you have a great opportunity to really "orchestrate" your office environment. Colors work like music: some notes harmonize and others conflict. The paint you choose will affect the look of fabrics near it and vice versa. The perception of one color changes when another is placed next to it. And, as we said before but can't say too often, the way the office is lit will affect the way the colors look.

Natural colors and textures never really go out of style (as long as they are appropriate and meet the needs of the office environment).

Task vs. Ambient Lighting

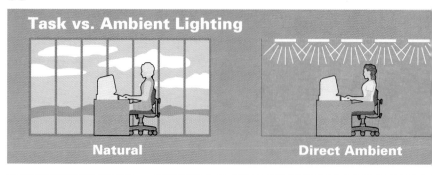

Natural **Direct Ambient**

What does ambient mean? It's from the French word *ambience,* which means atmosphere or environment. In office design, ambient refers to the general overall office environment, whether you're referring to light, heat, air-conditioning, or sound.

Layers of Light

"Don't read in the dark; you'll strain your eyes."

"You're too close to the television screen. Move back or you'll go blind."

Wait until that kid grows up, goes to work, and finds windowless offices, computer screen glare, and insufficient task lighting.

Lighting is important and complex. But we can subdivide the subject into basic components. Light may be your most expensive investment in terms of office design and may account for as much as 40% of your office's energy costs. In the long run, therefore, a well-planned lighting system can give you an efficient return.

People in offices need the right type of light to perform their work. There are four layers of light that affect the workplace. These are:

1. **Natural light**—daylight

2. **Ambient light**—low to medium general light, either direct or indirect. Typically provided by standard overhead "downlighting." Ideally ambient light should give a reflected, diffused, glareless light, which is most readily accomplished with indirect lighting.

3. **Task-oriented lighting**—at workstations, to create a pool of light on a given task. Task light should ideally provide for some degree of adjustment by the user.

4. **Accent lighting**—for bulletin boards, artwork, displays, to highlight plants, for areas remote from windows, or where reflected light from ambient fixtures is less than 20%.

Research has shown how it is possible to control and direct natural light into the office. Since lighting consumes by far the largest amount of energy in an office building, using the

S N R O
V K D Z
S N R V
O P Z Q
N K S O Z
R D V H C
S Q N R V D C K H
K O R Z S H V C N D
R O K V C Y Z H B N

Task   Indirect Ambient   Accent

most natural light possible is the easiest and most efficient way of cutting down energy costs. Some buildings have used light shelves not only to cut down on the glare of direct sunlight, but also to reflect light farther into the interior of an office space.

With the development of the **adjustable blind,** controlling daylight from the window is now possible. Direct light can be blocked, filtered, or re-directed by adjusting the angle of the blades. Colors on either side of the blind can be used either to absorb or reflect light. The blind can also act as a means of controlling solar heat. The lighter side can face outward, thereby reflecting heat out in summer; the darker side can face outward to absorb heat in winter.

Tinting the window glass also controls the amount of sunlight that will enter the office space. Reflective mirror glass not only keeps out light but reflects heat, as well.

Artificial Lighting

Artificial lighting has undergone significant changes in the past 15 years. Gone are the offices with rows of fluorescent ceiling tubes that imparted the garish ambience of an all-night supermarket to open-plan offices. In their place has arisen a concept known in the design world as **task/ambient lighting,** which involves a relatively subdued amount of background (ambient) light with concentrated, adjustable task lights where they're most needed. This change came about not only because of the energy crisis of the '70s, but also in recognition that even in offices brilliantly illuminated by fluorescent lights, workers were still using individual incandescent lights over their typewriters. With task lights, you control the direction and source of light, as well as contrast in the form of light and shadow. You cannot get lighting this specific from an even, overhead illumination system.

Why invest in a lighting system? Unless your office was built recently or is currently being constructed, your lighting system was designed for an era that is rapidly disappearing: the era of paper and pencil tasks that required "horizontal" seeing. Most people who work in offices now perform a combination of tasks involving paper and electronic equipment, and they perform them in close proximity, sometimes simultaneously. Many people, however, spend eight hours a day (and more) seated before a computer monitor. This requires "vertical" seeing. Lighting requirements are different for computer work.

Rather than designing to a predetermined number of footcandles per square foot, lighting should be designed for the work people need to do. This includes accounting for the color,

Different Types of Artificial Lighting

Ballast required ?	no	no	yes	yes
Color (on neutral surfaces)	red-yellow	yellow-white	bluish green	yellow
Typical use	home, accent	task, accent	corridor, warehouse	parking lot, street lighting
Start-up speed	instant	instant	slow	slow
Efficiency	low	low	medium	high
	Incandescent	**Tungsten Halogen**	**Mercury Vapor**	**High-Pressure Sodium**

Color Rendition of Artificial Light

In order for light to show objects in their true colors, it must contain light of all wavelengths. In other words, it must be white light, made up of all the colors of the rainbow. This is generally true of natural daylight (although near sunrise and sunset, natural light is primarily from the red-yellow end of the spectrum).

The problem with most artificial light sources is that they tend to contain light from a relatively narrow segment of the spectrum—which means they tend to distort our perception of colors. This affects different people to different degrees, but generally we are most comfortable working in light closest to natural daylight. None of us likes to have his or her complexions or clothing selections viewed in an unflattering light.

Color Temperature. In order to have an objective way of talking about the color rendition of different light sources, scientists developed the concept of "color temperature." The chart on the facing page shows the approximate color temperature of various types of artificial lighting, with natural light sources included for comparison.

The concept of color temperature is based on the fact that when a body, such as an iron bar, is heated, it will first glow a deep red, then a brighter red, then orange, and finally it will become white hot. The color of the light radiated—from red to blue-white—is thus related to the body's temperature. This is a theoretical rating: The color temperature of a light source is a convenient way to represent the *color* of the light; it has nothing to do with the actual temperature of the source.

Color temperature is expressed in degrees Kelvin—a scale in which each degree is equal to a degree Celsius, but the zero point is at absolute zero (minus 456° F).

placement, and intensity of light, as well as the tasks that are going to be performed. Today's office typically combines extensive reading with extensive automated tasks. Each requires a different kind of lighting. Reading requires a local task light that's bright enough to allow a reader to see written words clearly, yet diffuse enough to eliminate any glare on glossy paper. Computer work requires an overall ambient light that's soft, diffuse, glare-free, and positioned to eliminate reflections on the screen. The light level can be lower than for reading.

The goal is to `balance` surrounding ambient light with task light so that multiple tasks can be done comfortably in the same office, and by one person if needed.

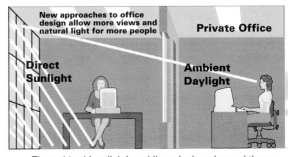

The task/ambient lighting philosophy has changed the way offices are designed. It is now typical to find private offices located next to the central core of the building rather than along the outside wall. Instead of granting access to daylight to only the lucky few in private offices and restricting the interior open spaces to a totally artificially lit environment, the current approach gives access to natural light to as many workers as possible. Open-plan workstations are often arranged in groups that allow circulation to occur near the perimeter windows, as well as around the central core. These days, private offices next to the core are provided with floor-to-ceiling glazed partitions that come furnished with adjustable blinds allowing for both daylight and privacy.

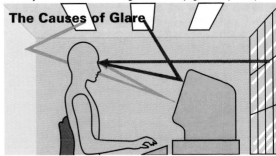

Metal Halide	Compact Fluorescent	Conventional Fluorescent		
		daylight	*cool white*	*warm white*
yes	yes	yes	yes	yes
greenish white	varies	blue-white	bluish	red-yellow
office, warehouse	task, accent	office	office	office
slow	instant	instant	instant	instant
high	high	medium-high	high	high

Most Common Lighting Problems in Offices

Glare manifests itself in different ways. *Direct Glare* is what you experience when you look directly into a light fixture, or into the high beams of an oncoming car. It's uncomfortable and can be blinding at times. *Reflected Glare* is what you experience when your computer screen, a glossy page, or other shiny surface reflects a light source back into your eyes. In addition to being uncomfortable, this type of glare makes the information on the page or screen unreadable.

Veiling Reflections

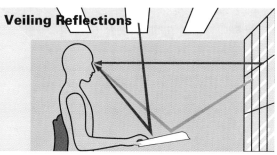

Veiling Reflections are a type of glare that occurs when the image of a light source or a brightly lit area is reflected in your screen. This bright, superimposed image obscures some or all of the information on the screen because contrast is reduced. Analogy: Try reading a glossy magazine near a bright light source. Solution: Change the angle of the magazine or move the light source.

Regardless of source, glare causes eyestrain, headaches, and slows down production. When properly applied, indirect ambient lighting can be very effective in eliminating glare. Inexpensive screens that block glare can also be installed on computer display terminals.

Cost—As a general rule of thumb, the less expensive a lamp is to buy, the more expensive it is to operate, according to the National Lighting Bureau. A lamp that costs more initially will almost always put out more light with less energy for a longer period of time than a cheaper one. If you want to keep costs down, look into "motion sensors" that turn off the lights when people aren't around. Cleaning light fixtures at least once every year or so will also make them work better and last longer.

Comparing Color Temperatures of Different Light Sources

If you are confused by the great variety of names used for the different kinds of fluorescent lamps available, look on the tube for a number followed by the letter *K*; this is its color temperature in degrees Kelvin. Then use this chart to see how it will compare to other kinds of lamps.

Color Temp. (°Kelvin)	Source
25,000°	
	Blue sky
10,000°	
8,000°	North light
7,500°	
7,000°	Overcast sky
6,500°	Daylight fluorescent
6,000°	Overcast sky
5,500°	
5,000°	Noon sunlight
4,500°	Cool white fluorescent
4,000°	White fluorescent
3,500°	Warm white fluorescent
3,000°	Tungsten halogen
2,500°	Incandescent
2,000°	Sunrise
1,500°	Candle flame

table of recommended illumination levels

activity	light in lux	foot-candles
drafting	1500-750	140-70
general office work	800-400	75-37
intermittent use (corridors, stairways, waiting rooms, etc.)	150-75	14-7
manufacturing— very fine work	5000-2500	465-230
manufacturing— fine work	2000-1000	185-90
general manufacturing	800-400	75-37

Sound Design Points to Remember

Sound can bounce off ceiling and walls

Sound-masking devices can help eliminate some distracting sounds

Barriers can stop many sounds

Sound easily travels from one workstation to another

Sound psychology

Adult subjects were given some complex puzzles to solve and a proofreading chore. In the background was a loud, randomly occurring distracting noise; to be specific, it was a "combination of two people speaking Spanish, one speaking Armenian, a mimeograph machine running, a desk calculator, a typewriter, and street noise—producing a composite, indistinguishable roar." The subjects were split into two groups. Individuals in one set were just told to work at the task. Individuals in the other were provided with a push button to turn off the noise, "a modern analog of control—the off switch." The group with the off switch solved five times the number of puzzles as their cohorts and made but a tiny fraction of the number of proofreading errors. Now for the kicker: "…none of the subjects in the off-switch group ever used the switch. The mere knowledge that one can exert control made the difference."

Tom Peters and Bob Waterman, *In Search of Excellence*

SOUND

We already know that a major problem in office design is balancing accessibility with privacy. Finding the right balance between an office that's too "soundproof" versus one that's too noisy is a challenge. A busy, active office where you're bombarded with sounds and activity can be stimulating and creative, but at times hinders work that requires concentration and confidentiality.

Two different sound issues need to be explored when designing office space: noise level and speech privacy.

Noise level—Is your building in the direct flight path of an international airport? Where is the mechanical equipment located? Is the executive washroom right next to the boardroom? How noisy are the printers? Who's got the loudest voice? How much quiet do workers require?

Total silence is not the optimal work environment. Every small cough would be distracting. Really noisy machines such as copiers and printers should be isolated if possible, but a level of noise should be maintained in the work area to prevent individual voices and noises from being intrusive.

Speech privacy—Do any of the workers require spaces for confidential conversations? Is there a place for telephone calls, employee reviews, or client negotiations? Being able to hear people's voices is very different from being able to distinguish what they're saying. There are acoustical solutions that allow bystanders to hear the sound of speech, but not the actual words. Your architect and furniture consultant can provide you with information about options.

The level of noise is a subjective perception based on the kind of work being done. If relative quiet is important for certain workers and their tasks, you can put them in properly designed offices, or move them far enough from noise sources to escape both the sound of machines and the necessary increase in voice volume of people working with or near those machines.

The main means for sound control:

Workstation distance—The farther away someone sits from a source of noise, the less he or she will hear it. Noisy departments such as the reception area, customer service or word processing should be as far as possible from the departments where people need to concentrate in quiet: editorial or accounting are good examples. The layout of workstations—especially the relationship between panels and openings—is just as important.

Barriers—Is there anything between the workstations and the sources of noise? Walls, partitions, and filing cabinets can impede or block noise. Sound bounces off hard surfaces, much like light off a mirror; it can also bend over the tops or around the sides of barriers. Higher barriers will keep more sound out but may also block vision. Holes in barriers—even uninsulated electric outlets—can let sound through.

Absorption—Is there anything to prevent the direct reflec-.tion of sound between or into workstations? Absorptive materi-als do this: some absorb distinct words and others absorb sound almost completely. Ceilings, absorptive wall coverings, carpets, and drapes can help absorb sounds. The Noise Reduction Coefficient (NRC) is the standard measure of sound absorption (ask your architect). Particular care should be taken in matching NRC and high-frequency sound absorption to open-plan needs. An acoustical consultant can give you specific recommendations.

Ambient sound—The overall level of background noise can cover up or "mask" disruptive or objectionable noises in a space. A key dropped on a factory floor is ignored, but can be an annoy-ance in a library. Sound-masking systems can be installed in the plenum space above the ceiling to provide overall "ambient sound." This kind of background sound can even cover up dis-tracting sounds like speech. Good sound masking should be turned on before people enter the building so they don't "hear" it. Have you ever noticed how annoying it is when the HVAC sys-tem is switched off and then flipped on while you're in the office? Good sound masking is invisible to the occupants, and music is not generally an effective substitute.

THE OF

THE OFFICE

The three topics and sections in this chapter are:

Then

Now

Next

No businessman these days dares to embark upon the journey of incorporation without first acquiring a computer so huge and so ominous as to strike terror into the software of its enemies.

Lewis H. Lapham, 1984

The reception room of the office of Francon & Heyer, Architects, looked like a cool, intimate ballroom in a Colonial mansion. The silver white walls were paneled with flat pilasters; the pilasters were fluted and curved into Ionic snails; they supported little pediments broken in the middle to make room for half a Grecian urn plastered against the wall. Etchings of Greek temples adorned the panels, too small to be distinguished, but presenting the unmistakable columns, pediments, and crumbling stone.

Ayn Rand, *The Fountainhead*

FORM, FUNCTION, AND FLEXIBILITY

Which is more important in office design: form or function? And why is it that the most effective office designs are often the ugliest, when tradition has taught us that effective is simple, and simple is elegant and beautiful? Since employer thinking has historically been geared to immediate and short-term results, the reaction was that function was all-important. If design was even discussed, the boss would call the "design" shots, designating who sat where and when, and on what. This was before design was recognized as an industry, much less a legitimate business concern. But as corporate image and employee involvement became issues and pyramids flattened, office appearance and comfort began to be seen as function issues, as well. This recognition coincided not so much with an aesthetic awakening, as a head-on collision with business needs.

It seems like forever, but do you remember the '80s? Corporate America became flashier, and the design of the workplace sleeker and bolder. Try to picture Trump Tower in New York. The office was the obvious showcase for success. Now picture the fantasy ad agencies portrayed on TV's "thirtysomething." Those hip offices looked more like high-tech Romper Rooms than

FICE

If there is one thing certain under automation it is that the job — even the bottom job — will change radically and often.

Peter F. Drucker, *America's Next Twenty Years*

Portion of all office space in US that was built during the '80s: one third.

Harper's Index, June 1991

One of the earliest office buildings is the Uffizi Museum in Florence, Italy. (*Uffizi* means "office" in Italian). It was built in 1560-1571 by Giorgio Vasari for Cosimo I de Medici to serve as the administrative headquarters for all of the Medici enterprises.

laces of business, and the behavior matched the furniture.
	While pool tables and basketball hoops may be an ex-
reme, most companies have gone to great lengths to achieve a
ealthier balance of form and function in the office. Employers
ave invested in high-tech equipment for speed and accuracy,
rgonomic furniture for comfort and health, and even art to
oothe computer-weary eyes. But "sensitivity" isn't really
nough these days.

1800

1810

1820

● **lithography invented**

● **carbon paper patented**

arithmometer ●
**calculating
machine**

1884: Architect William LeBaron Jenney designs the first office building with a steel skeleton, for the Home Insurance Company in Chicago.

1908: At 47 stories, New York's Singer Building, designed by Ernest Flagg, represents a quantum leap in height over any existing structure in Manhattan. The 600-foot-high building is visible from all over town, and is credited with starting the notion of the "tallest building in the world."

1959: Skidmore Owings & Merrill build the Union Carbide headquarters in New York City. This is one of the first high-rise office buildings conceived as a total system of coordinated parts. The lighting, layout, furniture, and storage cabinets were all designed in conjunction with the building's architecture. Many called it the "Rolls Royce of office buildings."

Today's "intelligent" office must be prepared for change, whether it's related to work habits or to technology. But change doesn't have to imply major renovations or moving into a new space. It simply means accommodating a third design element: flexibility.

The most effective office design anticipates and, in subtle ways, encourages innovation and reorganization within the company. **Flexibility** and change become part of both the office plan and the business plan so that, ideally, the workplace evolves with the company. While it may be that the organization and the business of the company shape the office on the macro level, the pulse behind change in office design—the one we all experience personally—is high-tech equipment.

There's a reason that electronics—as opposed to architects, designers, managers, or even employees—is the catalyst for change in office interiors. The impact of the electronic office is immediate, personal, and profound. Just think of the impact technology has on how people work. When many of us went to work at our first jobs, we hacked out memos and letters on electric typewriters. Multiple copies meant messy, cumbersome carbon paper or waiting in line to use the copy machine, which was usually jammed (adding another 10 minutes to the process). Today everybody simply boots up the computer, and voila: writing, editing, and printing with the touch of a few keys. Need more than one copy? That only takes a minute, and you never have to leave your desk.

● **postal system of carrying letters by weight and using gummed stamps introduced**

● **electronic telegraph patented**

rotary printing press ●

THEN

Offices haven't always been so versatile, however. And machines haven't always made so many demands on space.

In 1868, when Remington put the first practical typewriter on the market, all offices looked basically the same: a series of cramped rooms strung—tawdry-hotel style—along narrow, dimly lit corridors. The telegraph, introduced almost 25 years before, had little impact on office design. And even the telephone, which would make its debut in 1876, failed to alter the layout of the office, although it did much to alter business. The little closets off the hall eventually gave way to large-scale offices organized like factories—thank Henry Ford—with desks laid out by rows in a crowded room. The supervisor (a.k.a. Shop Foreman and Schoolmarm) sat behind a desk on an elevated pedestal at the front of the room, keeping a wary eye out for the employee whose mind wandered from the numbingly repetitive task at hand.

The factory model saw us through the Depression and two World Wars, but in the early '50s, when the IBM Corporation wowed the country with the first large-scale computer system, design wheels started to roll again.

Business was already starting to think bigger and better. A handful of skyscrapers had shot up during the '20s and '30s, but it is the post-war period that has been unofficially designated the era of the "glass box" office building. In 1959, when Xerox Corporation introduced the first convenient copier, many office layouts shifted to display this astonishing ultramodern luxury. In no time, this luxury become a necessity and the copying room became the office commons.

The '70s saw commercial development spread to the suburbs, where lower rent, cheaper land, easy freeway access, and an inexpensive and reliable labor force (housewives) were more attractive than anything offered downtown. The open plan became popular during this time; walls were torn down in an effort to open lines of communication and to abandon any hierarchy of status...except that, of course, men were still managers and women were still workers...and still nobody asked the employees what worked best for them.

In the late '70s, open-plan manufacturers realized that status *had* to be accommodated, so fancier fabric options, wood or fake-wood veneers, chrome, everything but tailfins was offered as an option, and space planners used office size and location as additional status symbols.

THEN

● elevators introduced

● gas lamps

Remington ●
typewriter

● first transatlantic communications
cable

● web printing press

For the first time in American history, a large number of the nation's adults have entered two of life's major passages at once: middle age and parenthood. Because many of these adults belong to a strategic segment of the population—the roughly 10 million managers and professionals between the ages of 35 and 45—their reaction to these passages is having a notable impact on American life: It signals a major shift away from the work-centered values of the '70s and '80s.

Utne Reader, July/August 1991

In a 1987 *Fortune* survey, conducted with New York's Bank Street College of Education, 30 percent of the men and 25.7 percent of the women said they had refused a new job, a promotion or a transfer because it would mean less time for their families. And almost 25 percent of both men and women sought a less demanding job so they could spend more time at home.

Executive Female, September/October 1987

A Famous Desk

The desk aboard the *USS Missouri* used in the signing of the peace treaty with Japan on 2 September, 1945 was a Steelcase desk.

And then, with the extravagant '80s, corporate offices took on a new shape. The open plan was modified with partitioned areas and enclosed offices that afforded some privacy. And technology became less of a marvel, almost taken for granted. It was a time of incredibly fast and profound changes in our attitudes toward the use of technology at the personal level. We had mastered the microwave oven and were ready to take on VCRs, fax machines, and cellular phones. Athletic clubs went high-tech with electronic bicycles, rowing machines and The Stairmaster. The '80s were a time of heightened contradictions: lavish offices and cut-throat competition, downsizing and lay-offs, outrageous salaries for green MBAs, homes that looked like design centers, and posh offices that could have been mistaken for private clubs.

Virtually everyone in today's office—from the chief executive who doesn't have a clue, to the receptionist who could probably be an equipment salesperson—has a computer at his or her desk and a fax machine within easy reach. Employers are no longer leery of sophisticated technical tools. Rather they're curious to know what the future holds in store and when it will be available. But how has this affected office design?

First of all, work has become more portable. Employees who find themselves working while on a plane, in a car, or at home have technology to thank—or blame, whichever the case may be. We even have portable copiers for home or light-duty small-business use. The result? Workers are logging in more odd and part-time hours. This translates into fewer people in the office at any given time. Researcher Franklin Becker describes offices in which whole classes of employees are out on most days, and the staff in the office is working somewhere other than at their desks.

Surprisingly, Becker's observation doesn't imply that the average *office* size is shrinking (although the work force needed at each office may be), nor are people working fewer hours. High-tech tools often take up more space than do the employees who operate them.

Offices should be redesigned to accommodate their various instruments and the creative uses employees have for them. One solution to the office-space problem is what is called the "nonterritorial" office. Group territories replace offices, desks—even storage systems—"owned" by individuals. Divide the office into spaces for specific projects or tasks. Thanks to automation, workers can carry information to whichever territory makes the most sense to work in—the library one day, and

● telephone invented   ● A.B.Dick introduces the mimeograph
    ● electric lights   ● employee time clocks
    ● steam heat
notype machine invented ●   ● ballpoint pens developed

                                 ● dictating machine introduced
    ● shift-key allows lowercase   suits become suitable ●
    letters to be typed   business attire

roject B's room the next. Sharing opens up more space for quipment and reduces the total overall equipment budget.

One reason the nonterritorial design is so effective is that ork patterns are less static than in the past.

It goes back to people. A generation of restlessness has left s mark on the professional world. People don't stay at jobs forver anymore, and when they are at work, the best of them don't ke sitting still and doing what they're told, at least not for long. dd this to the fact that information technology enables people interact from different buildings (and different cities and counies and different time zones, for that matter). Integrated information systems give everyone in the office access to a project, multaneously if desired. People want access; business wants sults; everybody benefits.

The "free-address office," first used by one of the rgest construction firms in the world, likewise challenges the gic behind "owning" a private office or desk. Tokyo-based himizu Corporation knew that fewer than half of its staff was sing the office on any given day, and so decided to conduct an xperiment.

Employees were given two choices: they could work at esks arranged front-to-front in the center of the room (the tradional arrangement) or at small workstations surrounded by panls. On coming to work, each person picked up a cordless telehone and a laptop computer, and wheeled a rolling pedestal ith his or her files to any unoccupied desk or workstation. The umber of desks was cut by about 30 percent and yet there was ctually more space available.

Whether the nonterritorial or the free-address office design right for your firm is for you to decide. The point is that work atterns are changing all the time, and the shape of the office nould change, too.

The hours that constitute the typical workday, for instance, re no longer etched in stone. Workers, especially baby oomers, are "downshifting," breaking the 8-to-5, Mondayrough-Friday routine. Early-bird types show up from 7 AM to 4 M, and still integrate work with night owls, who leave the office midnight. Electronic mail lets sales reps in California zip off a uestion to the home office in Cleveland, go home, and find the nswer waiting in the morning.

This kind of layout was used in the design of the Bank of America, Real Estate Division, in San Francisco by Robinson Mills & Williams, Architects. The understated 50,000-square-foot open-plan environment incorporates flexibility within permanently partitioned workstations so they can be rearranged (or "reconfigured" as designers say) to suit a variety of jobs.

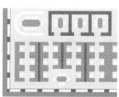

Note that conference rooms have curved glass walls near the four corners of the space. Circulation occurs along the perimeter, so that everyone has access to window views and daylight. Private offices are distributed around the core (the center of the office space).

39 percent of office employees nationwide work in private offices, 31 percent work in partitioned (open-plan) offices, and 29 percent in open areas (bullpens).

OEI Survey 1991

The reinvention of the corporation can be enabled by technology but can only be driven by people.

Shoshana Zuboff

Filofax introduced ●

neon lighting ●
invented in Paris

vacuum tubes invented ●

● **first metal office furniture**

coffee tables become popular ●
airmail establish●

microfilm first used in offices ●

air conditioning introduc●

NOW

In 1990 the *Wall Street Journal* reported that roughly 9.2 million Americans work at home at least part of the week, and predicted the ranks of these "telecommuters" would continue t● swell. (Please let this be true—those of us who travel a lot welcome the stay-at-home trend!)

Ironically, the office environment becomes even more important in this scenario. People who work part-time at home often look forward to the social stimulation of the office. They wa● to personally exchange ideas after sitting in front of a computer or taking care of the kids for half the week. A cubicle or isolated office may not cut it for telecommuters.

Not only are people working unconventional hours, but th● organization of the corporation is more elastic. Employers are willing to bend schedule rules for employees who make it wort● their time and money, and freelancers have become fixtures in many offices. *Fortune* magazine compares the arrangement— often called the "adaptive organization"—to a Busby Berkeley musical watched from above, where dozens of leggy dancers form a flower on stage, disband, and then regroup to form a fla● or fluegelhorn.

The core of this adaptive organization is made up of traditional departments such as accounting and sales. Like the piece● of colored glass in a kaleidoscope, these constantly changing teams, task forces, partnerships, and other informal groups spi● around the core staff, come together to do a job, and then break● up, with everyone going off to the next project.

With their newly found independence, employees may seem to disappear from sight in the office. Perhaps they're hole● up at home finishing a project, or slipping in and out at odd hours. By adding a few strategic inconveniences to the office de● sign, corporations can help to make sure these workers are at least somewhat visible. Central escalators and open central stai● cases slightly inhibit travel within the building, but the extra steps are worth it if they increase eye contact among the staff.

Chance encounters that lead to informal meetings on the stairs or near lounges are more comfortable in wide corridors and landings. People can ease in and out of traffic to discuss an● issue without making the kind of commitment implied by entering someone's office or a conference room.

At the Steelcase Corporate Development Center, for instance, "Corner Commons" placed at all four corners of the building encourage spontaneous meetings. Aetna Life and Cas● alty refers to its small commons rooms as oases. A strategically

Two-income families, flexible work hours, and a propensity to either work at home or bring work home from the office have led more than half of homeowners moving to a new house to set up a home office. Among that 50 percent, 46 percent of the 3,000 surveyed by *New Home* magazine say their home offices will be used to run a business, 39 percent for personal accounting and correspondence, and 13.1 percent to bring work home. Of these, 63 percent say they prefer a desktop PC, 16 percent an electronic typewriter, and 13 percent a laptop PC.

Personal Computing

What has happened to the briefcase?

Here's a gift suggestion for the peripatetic businessperson:

The latest briefcase models come complete with microphone/TV camera, color LCD, read/write optical CD storage, scanner, printer, cellular phone, modem, fax, miniature headset with earphone, microphone, keyboard, and tablet with stylus (removable, wireless, infrared).

1930 **1940** **1950**

● **fluorescent lights introduced** **transistor invented** ●
● **punch-card accounting machines introduced**
● **Underwood electric typewriter**
Charles & Ray Eames develop molded plywood chairs ●
DuPont synthesizes ● ● **welding process invented**
Nylon™

placed coffeepot might draw employees to an oasis and help to make informal, but often productive, conversations with others somewhat easier. White boards in the commons are useful for mapping out points.

Architect Niels Torp's Scandinavian Airlines building, just outside of Stockholm, features a central covered "street" embellished with trees, park benches, and cafes. Groups of offices and meeting rooms branch off from the sides in a sort of "Main Street" design. The common thoroughfare works well for the adaptive organization. Project teams can gather in meeting rooms to discuss a project and then easily return to their offices.

One way that corporations can provide these teams with the resources they need is to create project niches within the greater space. Five- to six-foot-high partitions within an open floor plan can be moved around to fit different group sizes. These "dedicated project rooms" should be equipped with lots of electrical outlets and lightweight desks and chairs.

Dedicated project rooms give temporary teams a sense of identity, and a place to interact. This is particularly important as organizations become more fluid. Give participants their own space, and, if possible, a desk, computer, and telephone for the duration of a project. As projects are completed and new ones begin, put up office signs that tell staff members what project they'll find in the space next. Signs that can be changed easily are an important design detail for the adaptive organization. A client we work with calls these signs "info stops." They're the office equivalent of a Parisian news kiosk.

Group spaces can be created with freestanding panels, but keep in mind, computer screens often link people more efficiently than a maze of partitions.

Instruments that lift the constraints of space and time—namely computers and fax machines—raise interesting questions about office design. For instance, does it matter where individuals are placed within the office if they're electronically accessible?

At Cypress Semiconductor, technology makes it easy for CEO T. J. Rodgers and other top managers to keep track of 1,500 employees without leaving their desks. Each Cypress employee keeps an updated list in his or her computer of 10 to 15 goals, with notes to the side indicating specifics like deadlines. Rodgers

MON

1950

Xerox copier introduced ●
● Rolodex introduced
Telex ●
introduced
halogen lighting ●
IBM Selectric typewriter ●

1960

● transistors begin to replace
vacuum tubes in computers
IBM Selectric II correcting typewriter ●
open-plan office systems first used ●
first IBM minicomputers ●
Xerox color copier introduced ●
8-bit microprocessor invented ●

1970

[Sherman] turned the corner, and there it was: the bond trading room of Pierce & Pierce. It was a vast space, perhaps sixty by eighty feet, but with the same eight-foot ceiling bearing down on your head. It was an oppressive space with a ferocious glare, writhing silhouettes, and the roar....The room was like a newspaper city room in that there were no partitions and no signs of visible rank. Everyone sat at light gray desks in front of veal-colored computer terminals with black screens. Rows of green-diode letters and numbers came skidding across.

The Bonfire of the Vanities,
Tom Wolfe

Americans now spend $20 million to $30 million each year treating hand problems, compared to just $10 million spent on head injuries.

San Francisco Business Times, 1990

The elevator

Optimum condition is a wait of no longer than 30 seconds. A good rule of thumb: One elevator per 45,000 gross square feet of building.

There are two kinds of elevators: hydraulic, an inexpensive system that is used in buildings up to five stories high; and traction (installed in buildings higher than five stories). These elevators can travel up to 1,000' per minute.

spends about four hours every week reviewing all the goals. The business could practically be supervised from Timbuktu, and Rodgers certainly doesn't have to worry about whether his offic is in the most central location.

Rodgers claims the system is never used to nag or pressur employees, but rather to alert upper management if goals aren' being met. If not, Rodgers asks how he can be of any help.

But Cypress Semiconductor's enlightened use of technol ogy isn't necessarily the norm.

Some companies operate on the premise that electronic eavesdropping increases productivity. Not surprisingly, these businesses coincide with our clichéd notions of the same com panies that provide poor service, unhappy employees, and un satisfactory results: many airlines, insurers, and telecommunica tions companies, among others, clock the time workers spend on computers or talking to customers over the telephone. The number of monitored employees reached 10 million in 1991, up from a handful only 10 years before. How this insult was sup posed to improve performance remains a mystery.

Corporations, thankfully, are bucking this foolish trend. Informal studies show that, in the long run, such close scrutiny slows down business and makes employees anxious. So much for market research. Intuition and common sense triumph again

Regardless of how technology is used to supervise em ployees, the fact remains that strategic seating arrangements ar less important than they once were. Location and office size don't always indicate status, or lack thereof. Instead of worrying over who sits where, bosses should ask themselves: Are my em ployees happy enough in their environment to give me the re sults we both need to stay successful? The business's overall well-being now takes precedence over where individuals sit. Companies that fail to keep up with "humane" design standards could wake up to discover their employees snatched away by more enticing offices, and more enlightened employers.

Today's Basics

What are the important things to remember when design ing the high-performance office?

For starters, furnish the office with ergonomically sound desks and chairs, for all the reasons we've discussed. Save space with the latest designs and in doing so, open up more room for high-tech equipment. Systems that save surface space or sit under the desk are hot items on the market.

1980   1990   2000

daisy-wheel typewriter   ● laser printers
  ● Xerox Star computer introduced
Post-It® notes   ● Apple Macintosh introduced
'smart' buildings developed ● ● first erasable optical drives
BM PC computer● ● Cellular phones test-marketed
  introduced   ● RISC technology developed
first FAX machines ●   for computer microprocessors

Systems furniture is particularly important in the open-plan design. Partitions provide some privacy, and workstations a "roosting" point. The first workstation was an L-shaped desk designed by George Nelson in 1947. Now there are any number of designs to choose from.

The office that depends heavily on electronics should use systems furniture designed to support the rat's nest of wires and cables connecting computers, printers, phones, and whatever else ends up in the space. Steelcase's CONTEXT® system and Haworth's Race system give users more control over their environments. The pieces open easily for wiring, repairs, and revisions. With CONTEXT®, cables can be moved without taking anything apart or interrupting work.

Systems furniture doesn't have to look boring just because it's consistent. Svelte curved panels, varied heights of partitions, and rich colors and materials can be as impressive as the mahogany-filled executive office of yesteryear, and certainly much more functional.

If you're trying to choose between systems and fixed-wall construction, keep in mind that systems lose some of their reconfigurability once they're strung together with wires and cables.

Many of the organizational forms and practices we have inherited from two centuries of industrial development are bankrupt...we are living through a period of profound historical discontinuity brought on by new markets, technology, and the changing nature of work for which different patterns of organization, behavior, and sensibility are required.

Shoshana Zuboff

As I see it, a healthy flow of information separates winning organizations from losers.

Arno Penzias, *Ideas and Information*

When is an Office Worker Not an Office Worker?

Technology not only resolves many potential communication problems, it can also make life in the office a lot more pleasant. One breakthrough: everyone can take home the wool sweaters stashed in their desks. With the right equipment and a well-engineered building, workers can adjust the temperature (by four to six degrees) and lighting within a small space, even at a cubicle. Today's office keeps workers comfortable around the clock and conserves energy.

Other amenities may call for renovation or rethinking.

Want to attract or keep productive employees who are also parents? Tolerant attitudes and a sense of the long-term goal are your best bets. Day-care centers don't hurt. Any office design that includes one is not only progressive, it's downright practical. A fitness facility is another sure-fire hit. They not only appeal to employees, but by keeping the staff in shape, cut down on sick days and medical bills. A cafeteria or kitchen is also in the company's best interest. If people don't have to leave the office for food, they might work longer hours and not turn a 30-minute break into an extended lunch/day trip. Some offices provide

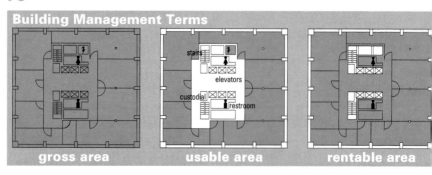

Building Management Terms

gross area   usable area   rentable area

(labels on middle diagram: stairs, elevators, custodial, restroom)

The typical executive office of the '80s, which measured a luxurious 15 by 20 feet, is now giving way to a more toned-down 15-by-15-foot space. To give a smaller office a more spacious feel, furnish it with a few large pieces instead of many small components. Also, consider bookcases hung above the desk or one floor-to-ceiling bookcase that looks built-in. Keep windows uncovered for as much natural light as possible; a dark office will feel even smaller than it is. And pare office plants, especially ficus trees and palms, so they will grow up, not out.

Working Woman, April 1991

banking and dry-cleaning services. If the latter is true, it follows that the office design should incorporate a large clothes closet for employees and guests. The point of these perks is really the message they convey.

A 10-person office may not be able to afford the expense; if you can't provide the facility, at least try to make it easier for your employees to easily get the things they need.

Address issues such as carpal tunnel syndrome (CTS) and exposure to video display terminals (VDTs). Furniture designed to relieve the symptoms is worth the investment and will probably save you legal as well as medical expenses down the road.

Some cities are considering legislation that requires companies to provide 15 minutes of alternative work for every two hours employees spend at a VDT. They also will be asked to provide adjustable swivel chairs, tables with ample leg space, glare filters, and discreet lighting. As cities and states pick up on these laws, support systems that allow terminals to be pushed back at least three feet will become a necessity. And so what if they do? A well-functioning office should allow for this extent of motion to begin with.

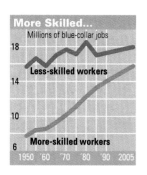

More Skilled...
Millions of blue-collar jobs

Less-skilled workers

More-skilled workers

18 — 14 — 10 — 6

1950 '60 '70 '80 '90 2005

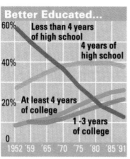

Better Educated...

Less than 4 years of high school

4 years of high school

At least 4 years of college

1-3 years of college

60% — 40% — 20% — 0

1952 '59 '65 '70 '75 '80 '85 '91

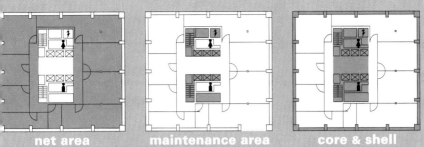

net area   maintenance area   core & shell

The Only Constant

In what direction is the shape of the office headed? We've all seen "Star Trek" and can dream about the day when we're able to "beam" ourselves back and forth from work. But more realistically, the shape of the office depends on changing technology and demographics.

As the population ages, so does its work force. And just as the number of working mothers went up during the '80s and '90s, the number of workers over 50 is bound to increase by the turn of the century. Competent workers may develop hearing problems or have trouble seeing. They may not be as agile as before. Technical developments will, no doubt, keep abreast of this trend. And the concept of telecommuters will become positively entrenched.

What if, to accommodate telecommuters, companies went back to the open-plan office but gave it a twist: at the push of a button, panels would drop down from the ceiling to create spaces within the larger office? This way the office could be reconfigured as needed, perhaps on a weekly basis.

Experts predict a sweeping trend toward miniaturization, especially of computers, that will push designers to come up with new concepts for furniture and workstations. Canon Inc. has already developed the Navigator HD-40, an all-in-one telephone, fax, answering machine, and personal computer and printer. This futuristic "office-in-a-box" could be the perfect solution to desktop clutter.

As equipment shrinks in size and storage becomes less necessary (but beware the paperless-office myth) smaller, light-weight desks, constructed of cardboard or an equally portable material, may find their way into the office. Such desks could be moved around easily for different projects. And if they cost less, companies could sink more money into chairs, which really seem to affect health and performance.

Not only is equipment growing smaller, but the size of the individual office is about five square feet less than it was 10 years ago. If this trend continues—as is expected—furniture that is sleek and multifunctional will prevail over bulky wooden desks. When people want their space personalized, they can begin to do so in ways no office planner could have dreamed of a generation ago.

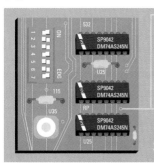

Infrared Sensors turn on lights when movement is detected

Electronic Sec involves a car or programmable code, may connect to an internal elect system. State-of-the-art wire " highways" will allow all building sys to operate from a main computer

Smart Buildings: Thinking For Yo

The future isn't what it used to be.

Who would have guessed, for instance, that companies as diverse as a worldwide delivery service and a California police force would choose pen-based computers over traditional carbon copies for accurate record keeping? Pen-based computers have been around for years, but have only recently come into common use. United Parcel Service was among the first to adopt the technology, equipping their delivery men and women with unwieldy Atlas-sized Diad Systems that could record signatures. We say unwieldy because while the technology was an upgrade, the machine's size is an extra burden for UPS employees laden with heavy packages. But it doesn't take long for better mousetraps to be developed.

The San Jose, California police force, which is testing the use of pen-based computers for field reporting, had nothing but good things to say about the technology as of spring 1992. Their police cars are equipped with data terminals that receive dispatch information about emergency calls; the officers take their pen-based portables "on call" with them to write up their reports on site. "The advantage is that the computers convert everything we write to type," explains Officer Tony Weir. The technology these officers are testing out is the Grid Pad, which is the size of a clipboard and weighs about four pounds, as well as the slightly larger and heavier Momenta. In either instance, technology is being used to support the immediacy and complexity of information in a useful, responsive way. And no example better demonstrates the needs of the mobile, nontraditional office and employee.

As far as the typical office goes, however, pen-based computers have yet to carve their niche. One technological development that has made phenomenal headway is the seemingly ubiquitous voice mail, an invention that everyone loves to hate. Like answering machines and call-waiting, which are incredibly useful but often annoying, voice mail enables you to get in touch with someone by leaving a message. The frustrating aspect of voice mail is the fact that you hear a recording of the person's voice and yet can't get through to the person—you can only leave a message. The good news is, you *can* leave a message. And, just as e-mail has made some people braver communicators, so, too, voice mail can at least give you the perception you're getting through to the people who previously employed the "secretarial screen defense." Of course, there's no guarantee your call will be returned.

A big complaint about voice mail is that many receptionists use it as a first rather than last resort and put callers through to the recording without letting on that so-and-so isn't in (and

Smart Air Conditioners
adjust temperature to the number of people in the office and send less heat to hallways and basements

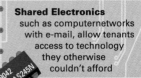

60 65 70 75 80

Smart Elevators
go to the busiest floors
at rush hour, may wait
five minutes for the rider,
and shut down automatically
when smoke alarm is activated

Shared Electronics
such as computernetworks
with e-mail, allow tenants
access to technology
they otherwise
couldn't afford

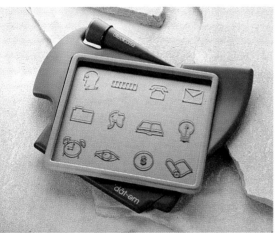

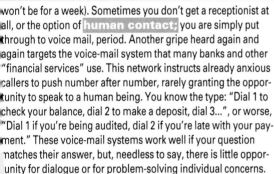

won't be for a week). Sometimes you don't get a receptionist at all, or the option of **human contact;** you are simply put through to voice mail, period. Another gripe heard again and again targets the voice-mail system that many banks and other "financial services" use. This network instructs already anxious callers to push number after number, rarely granting the opportunity to speak to a human being. You know the type: "Dial 1 to check your balance, dial 2 to make a deposit, dial 3...", or worse, "Dial 1 if you're being audited, dial 2 if you're late with your payment." These voice-mail systems work well if your question matches their answer, but, needless to say, there is little opportunity for dialogue or for problem-solving individual concerns.

The greatest voice-mail problem is the impression it leaves on the caller, who inevitably begins to assume the person who can't be reached simply never comes to work. Or worse, that the person is deliberately avoiding a conversation. Oddly, the reason most companies give for installing voice mail is that they want to free up their staff for more "productive" tasks. The cause is noble, but if these employees are so available, why do the customers feel as though service is degenerating rather than improving? Companies should be very specific about the productivity goals voice mail is intended to meet, and those goals should not include more time spent for intra-company communication to the detriment of service to clients and customers.

But voice mail has many redeeming qualities. For instance, many operations are so advanced that the caller can retrieve a message at the last minute if he or she decides it wasn't exactly appropriate. And callers don't have to depend on busy receptionists to take in-depth or personal messages. Perhaps the best advantage, however, is for the cold caller; you can relay a lot of information about yourself or your business on a tape that says "You may leave a message of any length."

Look Who's Talking

Office telephones that feed off a computer's power can provide even more service. Northern Telecom's Meridian TeleCenter system enables desktop computers to take phone calls and written memos. A computer can be programmed to route calls from certain outside numbers directly to you and to reroute all others to your assistant; preferred callers are saved having to go through a receptionist, and experience the "good feeling" of being important enough to be granted direct access.

The system also makes it possible to give verbal instructions via computer. This is a step up from dictation. Say the letter you've asked your secretary to type requires complex instructions; with Meridian TeleCenter, you can program a message to your assistant that flags specific areas (a flag actually appears on screen) and the typist is able to play back your recorded message and incorporate your instructions into the final text.

Along the same lines, Apple Computer's Casper program actually takes verbal commands. In other words, instead of typing in commands, you can talk to your computer and tell it to schedule appointments or to file names and phone numbers. At this rate, bosses will be required to be as organized and articulate as they have historically demanded of their support staff. These **"silicon secretaries"** promise the office scenario plenty of opportunities for reassessing roles and relationships.

Videoconferencing is another open-ended technological development. The concept is based on television and dates back at least as far as the 1964 World's Fair. Office meetings between groups or individuals are now on the air. Videoconferencing is particularly useful among companies that are closing complicated deals or merging and don't see the value of spending the time or money to be together for every decision or announcement. Rooms with 25-inch monitors, microphones, fiber-optic phone lines, and video processors are equipped and rented out by telecommunications companies such as AT&T and PacBell; the rates range between $200 and $3,000 US an hour (the pricier represents trans- or intercontinental video-conferences). Compare those prices to the sometimes excessive amounts a corporation might spend on travel, meals, and hotels for the same meetings. Executives who are using videoconferencing feel it is more reasonable and adds that much more value to the well-planned personal visit. Some companies are so bullish on the technology, they've installed videoconference rooms within their own offices.

In 1992, there were more than 2,000 private videoconference sites in the United States alone. Picture-Tel Corporation leads US production of videoconferencing equipment, with most of their units installed in the offices and boardrooms of *Fortune* 100 companies. Whoever sits at the desktop control panel of their System 4000 unit can make the camera zoom and pan, following the speaker around the room if necessary.

One video feature that has caught on allows a user to record a video message or presentation of up to 20 minutes, which can be stored for later use or sent to branch offices around the world. Again, technology is molding people's skills. An effective meeting manager is now called upon to be an effective video producer and to understand more than ever before that the medium influences the message.

Virtual reality, the technology that enables users to manipulate objects in a computer-generated world, signifies the best of what's to come. In a business application, engineers in different cities using goggles and gloves can work simultaneously on, say, the design of an airplane or an automobile. The gloves they wear are linked to workstations in a high-speed network; every time a hand turns a wrench or adjusts a part, the movement is mirrored on screen, and elicits comments from the other end.

The technology may sound too far out for the average office, but a number of industries have already put it to practical use. Japan's NEC Corporation predicts that engineering teams in Europe, the United States, and Japan will use powerful computers to share **"virtual workbenches"** to design cars on a regular basis by 1995. As the technology is fine-tuned, architects can look forward to "walking through" a building before they've broken ground. They will actually be able to move furniture around and rearrange offices. And so, we've come full circle from the reality of people and space to the virtual reality of imagination and design. The best offices of the future will be those that propose the most workable solutions to these equally important needs.

INVEN

Here's a checklist of questions you can ask yourself to help determine your office's needs and how they can best be met

PERFORMANCE

How does your office review and reward people's **performance?**

How does your office motivate people to work effectively?

Is a career path available for all employees?

Does your office provide enough interaction between people? Between workers and managers? Managers and executives? Workers and executives? Workers and workers? Different departments? Between the company and the public?

How many workers does your office support? What kind of workers are they? What kinds of work do they perform?

What are the office's public and private realms?

Are the offices too small to be effective?

What kind of management style is employed in your office? Does management withhold information in an attempt to consolidate power? Do managers circulate often? Should they?

Is work team-oriented? If so, does your office physically support teams getting together to meet and work together? Do systems allow different people to communicate easily about projects or shared work?

Are managers or executives easily accessible (open-door management)?

Which projects are defined as independent tasks, which as sequential tasks? Does your office group these workers together? Does your office physically support different kinds of work?

PROXIMITY

What arrangements does your office have to organize people in terms of **proximity?** How flexible is the plan?

Can people be moved easily? Does the cost and potential upheaval of a move discourage rearranging people in a more effective way?

How are teams or departments organized? Are those that share similar functions grouped together (such as a secretarial pool) or are people placed next to those whose work they support (such as a manager)?

Does design facilitate communication between different departments?

Does your office plan promote movement? Is it easy to get from office to office? From entrance to exit? Does it promote action?

Does everyone have adequate access to equipment such as copiers, computers, fax machines, and telephones?

Is the restroom nearby or situated on the other end of a long trek? Does everyone have reasonable access to the lunchroom and a water fountain?

Do people have a place to make a private phone call?

Is there a place for quiet work? Is it difficult to schedule the use of these places?

What are your office's security needs? Are they being adequately met? Is trash disposed of or is it shredded? Are people screened as they enter and leave sensitive areas?

Is there more security than is really necessary? Is the attitude imposed on your office unreasonably suspicious? Do your employees feel like they're constantly under surveillance?

Are needs being met redundantly (a little redundancy is good, but too much can be a waste)?

POWER

What kind of organizational structure does your company have?

Do people's titles match their job descriptions?

How is rank or position in your office expressed? By private offices? Location? Furnishings?

Does your office express an air of exclusivity? Does it encourage creativity and ingenuity?

Do employees have access to the information they need to do their work?

Do employees have a choice in their furniture, equipment, or surroundings?

Do they have a say in the how their environment is changed? Temperature? Art? Colors? Materials?

What does everyone involved think about their offices and work space?

STORAGE

How does your office handle and retrieve information? Is information kept on computer disks or in paper form?

What types of documents does your office handle? Electronic? Fax? Paper? Forms?

Are your facilities capable of handling the amount of documentation that they do? Are they capable of handling quantities consistent with projected growth for your organization?

Where do documents originate in your office? Fax machines? Mail? Interoffice memos? Reports from headquarters or from field offices?

Do you know where the mailroom is? Do you know who handles the mail, sorts it, and delivers it?

How long does it take a letter to move through your mailroom? Is it fast enough for your business needs?

Are present typewriters, computers (both hardware *and* software), and printers adequate to handle the needs of your office? Do you know where to find similar services in case your machines break down and you're at the end of a deadline? Do you know where to find services such as binding, color copying, special materials, and typesetting if you have an unusual project that requires capabilities you hadn't planned on?

Are documents copied to extremes both in paper and electronic forms? Do copies and other document forwarding procedures create too much information and too many documents in the information stream? Are they necessary to effectively keep everyone informed and updated?

Does your office have a recycling program?

How is the path and amount of paper flow in your office monitored and billed?

How much mail traffic does your office receive? How much does it generate?

How much phone traffic (both incoming and outgoing) does your office deal with?

Are the facilities and jobs that manage and respond to these administrative needs adequate? Do they receive enough respect and attention? Do they have the proper equipment for efficient management?

How are your files organized? From A-Z? By project or other category? By location? By urgency or other continuum? By time? In more than one way? Do the indexes to your files allow you to find information quickly from a variety of different organizational methods or key words?

How often are your files updated? How often are references or cross-references to these files updated?

Do you keep archives of old documents? Are they on electronic media or in paper form? Who are your office's **archivists**? Do you have off-site archives in case of a disaster in your office?

What are the different legalities concerning how many documents, what type or condition, and how far back you have to keep records for your business?

Do workers have enough storage for the work they do? Is there adequate storage space for shared files and information?

Do employees have space to store personal things (a change of clothes, a second pair of shoes, a coat, a lunch)?

SURFACES

What type of desks do your employees have?

How do you provide for pin-up and display material?

How do you arrange both formal and informal presentations? Pin-up boards? Audiovisual screens? White boards?

What kinds of computers does your office use (if at all)? What are your plans for the future regarding computer equipment and printers?

What kinds of networks do you use? Are they fast enough?

Are you using e-mail? If not, could it facilitate better information exchange?

What kinds of monitors are your employees using? Do they have adequate glare prevention? Are they beginning to flicker and cause eyestrain?

Are the workstations in your office properly designed and adjusted to fit your employees? Do your employees complain of backaches or wrist problems?

Do your workers take adequate breaks to relieve stress on their muscles, hands, and eyes?

Does your office have a high incidence of absenteeism and medical problems? Could this be due to the design (or lack thereof) of its workstations?

Are there enough work surfaces to accommodate both the everyday workflow and the occasional overload?

Do you have a project room, war room, or "solutions" room to accommodate intense project sessions and ongoing project work?

Is your conference room comfortable? Is it big enough?

SEATING

Are your office seats comfortable?

Is the choice of chair based on cost, style, function, or a combination of all three? Who makes these chairs?

Do people have a chance to get up and flex their muscles?

Are these chairs on stable bases? Do they swivel? Do they support the body adequately for all tasks being performed? Do they avoid pressure points when reclined?

THE PLACE

What is the comfort level of your office? Do people feel secure? At ease? Hurried? Under surveillance?

Is the HVAC system properly maintained? Is it recirculating smoke and other irritants?

Is there excess sneezing and illnesses in your office (these could be indicators of poor air quality)?

Do you have appropriately designed furniture to help minimize repetitive strain injuries? Do your work practices allow sufficient breaks for at-risk workers? Do you give them adequate training?

Is there handicapped access through your office? To the lunchroom and files as well as the restroom and workstations?

SIGHT

What image does your office project? Does this image match the kind of business your office does? Does the **image** area of your office end with the reception area and main conference area?

Who designs your office? The partners? Individual employees? The office manager? An interior design firm? Your spouse? No one?

Are there enough eye breaks throughout the office to offer visual relief? Are there any?

Are there any views? Can they be shared by everyone?

LIGHT

What lighting system does your office have? Overhead fluorescent? Incandescent? Task/ambient?

Who designed your lighting system? The landlord? The office manager? An outside consultant?

Are you making good use of natural light? Do you rely too much on artificial light? Could you save money by installing more efficient fixtures and bulbs?

Are glare and veiling reflections a problem for your employees? Could you benefit from glare-free indirect ambient lighting?

SOUND

What is the noise level in your office?

Is there adequate acoustic privacy? Is it too noisy? Too quiet?

Is work compromised by lack of privacy?

Where can an employee make a confidential phone call? Where do you hold confidential conversations and interviews?

Can you install barriers to block sound? Can you upgrade ceilings or install acoustical wall coverings to absorb sound?

Would a sound-masking device (either electronic or something like a fountain or a waterfall) help decrease sound distractions?

BIBLIOG

BOOKS

Bandrowski, James F.
*Corporate Imagination Plus:
Five Steps to Translating
Innovative Strategies into
Action*
The Free Press, 1990
This provocative book explains how to develop imaginative strategies and then get your organization to implement them. Especially interesting are the nuggets of information gathered through interviews with innovative corporate executives at Apple Computer, Charles Schwab, and Gensler & Associates.

Becker, Franklin
The Total Workplace
Van Nostrand Reinhold, 1990
The illustrations in this book are probably more confusing than helpful, but if you're interested in understanding how space interacts with people and affects progress in the office, take a look at Becker's work.

**Bradford, Peter and
Barbara Prete**
Chair
Thomas Y. Crowell, 1978
Based on the lecture series "The Evolving Chair" sponsored by the Cooper-Hewitt Museum in New York City in 1976. Eight renowned furniture designers share, in words and photographs, their insights and ideas about chair design in this clever, artistic book.

**Brill, Michael with
Stephen T. Margulis and
BOSTI**
*Using Office Design to
Increase Productivity*
Workplace Design and Productivity, Inc., 1985
This two-volume work presents the results of a large-scale, long-term research project on the affects of various aspects of the office environment on the employee's performance and ease of communication. The second volume provides a set of design guidelines for high-performance offices, and suggests useful procedures to better understand offices in the design process.

**Crane, Robin and
Malcolm Dixon**
The Shape of Space
Van Nostrand Reinhold, 1991
Created by designers for designers, this book is 95% drawings, but they're extraordinarily helpful and comprehensible drawings. And while *The Shape of Space* is probably more appropriate for professional architects and designers, the illustrations are fun to look at for ideas about space planning (and it deals strictly with offices).

**Diffrient, Niels with
Alvin R. Tilley and
Joan C. Bardagjy**
Humanscales 1/2/3
Humanscales 4/5/6
Humanscales 7/8/9
MIT Press, 1974
A detailed and in-depth reference on many aspects of ergonomics. These three sets of humanscale data form an irreplaceable resource for designers and architects.

RAPHY

OFFICE SYSTEMS

Designs for the Contemporary Workplace

Edwards, Sandra and the editors of *Industrial Design* magazine
Office Systems: Designs for the Contemporary Workplace
PBC International, Inc., 1986
A real coffee-table book with glossy paper, four-color photographs, and ideas about office design by the people who have seen and read it all. The first section showcases furniture systems by 36 top designers, and the back of the book provides an in-depth look at the options available for seating, desks and tables, lighting, and accessories.

Garson, Barbara
The Electronic Sweatshop: How Computers are Transforming the Office of the Future into the Factory of the Past
Simon and Schuster, 1988
This book looks at the nature of automation among white-collar workers and shows how computers are being used to transform secretaries, executives, and other professionals. From McDonald's to Shearson Lehman, Barbara Garson discloses how technology has altered familiar companies.

Graf Klein, Judith
The Office Book
Quarto Marketing Limited, 1982
This book may be 10 years old, but the information is still relevant. A practical guide to planning, designing, and decorating the modern office, it covers everything from choosing a desk to revamping the reception area. Written especially for the office planner with limited design experience.

Greig, Michel
The Visual Factory: Building Participation Through Shared Information
Productivity Press, Inc., 1991
Michael Greig answers seemingly simple questions such as: "How should one set up a bulletin board?" to illustrate ways in which information can be made "commonly available and understandable at a glance to all who view it." His view is that the sharing of the information among management and staff "brings new light and life to the culture of the workplace."

Hackman, J. Richard, editor
Groups That Work (and Those That Don't): Creating Conditions for Effective Teamwork
Jossey Bass Publications, 1991
The authors of this collaborative book analyze seven distinct types of work groups to determine why some succeed while others fail, examining the factors and conditions that foster good team performances with high-quality outcomes. The work

groups range from top-management teams to athletic teams and theater companies. Find out the five most common mistakes made by group leaders and learn how to avoid such pitfalls.

Hine, Thomas
Facing Tomorrow
Alfred A. Knopf, 1992
Examining what has been and predicting what the future can be, Thomas Hine (the author of *Populuxe*) concludes that "the vision of the future provided by technology *looks* great, but may fail to nourish us in more profound and subtle ways." Hine is concerned with making sense of what's to come, particularly in the workplace. One chapter addresses the use of technology, touching on everything from robots to virtual reality.

Kleeman, Walter B.
Interior Design of the Electronic Office
Van Nostrand Reinhold, 1991
This book addresses design issues from office wiring to choosing a chair, spelling out design methods based on the latest research in such disciplines as architecture, ergonomics, and information technology. Down-to-earth explanations should enable any reader to grasp such seemingly lofty design concepts as computer-aided office design.

Kliment, Stephen A.
Architectural Graphic Standards, student edition
John Wiley & Sons, 1989
Highly detailed illustrations of everything from door-closing devices to work sinks. Compiled for the architectural student, but also useful for the amateur designer.

Koestenbaum, Peter
Leadership: The Inner Side of Greatness
Jossey-Bass Publishers, 1992
Business consultant and philosopher Peter Koestenbaum answers this compelling question: What makes a leader great? In brief, his book deals with the personal side of business leadership, revealing what managers must know, learn, and be in order to become truly effective leaders.

Penzias, Arno
Ideas and Information
Touchstone, 1989
This Nobel Prize-winning physicist writes here about the relationship between words and microchips. An intriguing guide to the ways technology is shaping the modern world and redefining business. If you've been struggling to get a grasp of how developments in computer technology have shaped the past 30 years, definitely read this book.

Pilzer, Paul Zane
Unlimited Wealth: The Theory and Practice of Economic Alchemy
Crown Publishers, Inc., 1990
Paul Zane Pilzer's thesis that wealth is no longer produced by controlling scarce resources because technology has virtually done away with scarcity is illustrated in the careers of entrepreneurs such as H. Ross Perot and Sam Walton. This book predicts what the immediate advances in technology will mean to individuals, businesses, and society.

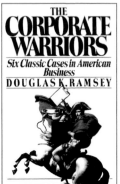

Ramsey, Douglas K.
The Corporate Warriors: Six Classic Cases in American Business
Houghton Mifflin Company, 1987
Douglas Ramsey's premise is that "modern business is a brutal battlefield and there are crucial lessons to be drawn from military strategy." He examines such legendary corporate battles as those between Coke and Pepsi, People Express and other airlines, and Ted Turner and other networks to illustrate ways in which business wars are calculated and waged.

ARTICLES

Brown, John Seely
"Research That Reinvents the Corporation"
Harvard Business Review (January-February 1991)

Deutschman, Alan
"Pioneers of the New Balance"
Fortune (20 May 1991)

Dumaine, Brian
"The Bureaucracy Busters"
Fortune (17 June 1991)

Farmanfarmaian, Roxane
"Old Office, New Office"
Working Woman (April 1987)

Freiman, Ziva
"The Office of the Present"
Progressive Architecture (September 1990)

Hopkin, Jane
"The Humane Touch"
Design (December 1990)

Laporte, Suzanne B.
"How to Make a Teeny Office Seem Bigger"
Working Woman (April 1991)

Mamis, Robert A.
"What to Do About Carpal Tunnel Syndrome"
Inc. (May 1991)

Semler, Ricardo
"Managing Without Managers"
Harvard Business Review (September-October 1989)

Specht, Pamela Hammers
"Information Sources Used for Strategic Planning Decisions in Small Firms"
American Journal of Small Business (Spring 1987)

"Can Research Reinvent the Corporation?"
Harvard Business Review (March-April 1990)

GLOSS

access:
The points where electrical equipment can be plugged into the furniture's distribution system, and where cables are made available for connecting data/telecommunications equipment.

adaptive organization:
Model that allows certain tasks—rather than individuals—to shape the organization of a company.

ambient lighting:
The general level of illumination throughout a room or area.

ambient sound:
Background sound composed of all sounds in an area.

ampere:
A unit used to measure the amount of electrical current flowing through a circuit.

application program:
A tool to manipulate information and help computer users. When people refer to a "program," they really mean an "application."

artificial intelligence (AI):
The study of how to make computers do things that, traditionally, people do better. Certain software has aspects that allow computers to "think," "learn," and make decisions or mimic lower levels of human intelligence.

American Standard Code for Information Interchange (ASCII):
A system used to represent letters, numbers, symbols, and punctuation as bytes of binary symbols (1s and 0s).

assembly line:
Method of production attributed to automobile manufacturer Henry Ford in which a product is made by several people who work on distinct and separate tasks and then pass the product on to another person until it is completed.

baby boomers:
Population of 76 million "achievers" born between 1946 and 1964.

baby busters:
Generation born between 1964 and 1984; smaller population than the baby boomers; is less corporation-oriented, more entrepreneurial.

ballast:
Device that modifies incoming voltage and current to provide the circuit conditions necessary to start and operate electric discharge lamps.

bit:
The smallest unit of data in a computer (or any digital machine) symbolized as either a 1 or a 0 and representing a physical property in the computer circuit or storage media.

bridge:
A device that enables computer users to connect networks.

bull pen:
An office where several people share one large open space. It is not uncommon for dozens, even hundreds, of workers to sit in a bull pen at desks laid out in neat rows. This organization offers little or no privacy.

byte:
A group of eight bits used to encode a single letter, number, or symbol.

cableway:
An opening in a work surface that allows access to cords or cables from below, or mounting of an electrical receptacle or telephone jack. Cableways are standard with removable plastic grommets.

candlepower:
Basic unit for measuring light from a source in a given direction.

carpal tunnel syndrome (CTS):
Repetitive strain injury that may affect people who make identical motions with their hands throughout the day. If untreated, CTS can cause serious medical damage.

cathode ray tube (CRT):
An electronic display that shoots electrons through a tube to a phosphorescent screen (like a television set) to display information.

cellular phone:
A portable telephone that uses a system of satellites, service area cells, and transceiver stations to maintain phone system service.

central processing unit (CPU):
Also called a processor; the basic "chip" that processes the instructions in a computer. A CPU consists of a logic unit, a control unit, a clock, and memory. Often used for the box containing these elements.

chip:
Small piece of silicon that is a complete semiconductor device or an integrated circuit.

churn rate:
The amount of employee turnover at a business during a given year.

cluster:
Physical grouping of workstations that share one or more panel runs.

compact disk-read only memory (CD-ROM):
A format for storing information digitally on a compact disk.

computer-aided design (CAD):
A category of computer application programs used to design and develop products and buildings.

computer conferencing:
Also known as electronic conferencing or computer-based text messaging. This is when two or more people communicate from different locations via computer.

corporate pyramid:
Classic way of organizing a company with the chairman of the board and the president at the top and all other employees stacked in a broadening shape beneath them.

data highway:
A system that connects individual microprocessors located throughout a building and monitors the changing interior conditions within the building. Ultimately, the data highway adjusts all systems—whether mechanical, electrical, communication, transportation, heating, cooling, safety, or security—to optimum performance levels.

diffused lighting:
Light that isn't coming from any particular direction.

disk:
The magnetic medium on which a computer stores information.

disk drive:
The mechanism that holds the disk, retrieves information from it, and saves information on it.

dots per inch (DPI):
A measure of resolution or detail used for screens (monitors) and printers.

e-mail:
Nickname for electronic mail, an electronic "memo" system that lets people exchange messages or documents on their computer screens.

ergonomics:
The study of human comfort and effectiveness in relation to equipment and furniture design.

expert system:
An area of artificial intelligence that allows a computer to make decisions based on a set of organized rules created from a knowledge base about a particular subject.

facilities management:
The coordination of all efforts related to the planning, design, and management of an organization's physical resources.

facsimile machine:
Better known as a fax machine. Using telephone technology, documents are quickly and inexpensively transmitted from one office to another.

file server:
A device that combines controller software and mass storage to allow computer users to share common files and applications across a network.

footcandle:
A unit of measurement of the amount of light falling onto a surface.

frame:
Inner support structure of upholstered furniture; may be wood, metal, or plastic.

free-address office:
Office arrangement in which all personal spaces are eliminated in favor of employees picking up their supplies at a front desk upon arriving and then choosing a temporary work area each day.

furniture integrated ambient light (FIAL):
Ambient office lighting that is mounted on systems furniture.

gigabyte:
A unit of memory measure equal to 1,024 megabytes or 1,048,576 kilobytes.

glare:
A discomforting or disabling condition that occurs when a high-brightness source contrasts with a low-brightness background, making it difficult for eyes to adjust.

gloss:
The degree to which a coating is able to reflect images.

graphic-user interface (GUI):
A type of interface between the user and computer that represents processes and objects as visual symbols in a two-dimensional environment.

grayscale monitor:
Any monitor capable of showing levels of gray and not just black or white.

groupware:
Software that allows several people working on the same things to better interact and communicate.

hard disk:
A disk drive that has the non-removable disk permanently encased. Sometimes called a fixed disk.

hardware:
Anything physical about the computer that you can see or touch.

HVAC:
Stands for heating, ventilating, and air-conditioning systems.

hypertext:
Also called hypermedia; software that allows users to explore and create their own paths through written, visual, and audio information. Capabilities include being able to jump from topic to topic at any time and follow cross-references easily.

indirect lighting:
Lighting directed upward to be reflected off ceiling and walls to create soft, glare-free ambient illumination. Luminaires can be hung from the ceiling, mounted on furniture, or freestanding.

infotech:
Information technology.

integrated services digital network (ISDN):
A digital switching system that allows data, image, video, and voice transmission via a single phone line.

ischial tuberosities:
The two small "sitting bones" in the buttocks.

kilobyte (K):
A unit of memory measure equal to 1,024 bytes.

knocked-down (KD):
Furniture shipped from the factory in parts to be assembled by the customer or retailer.

lamp:
The lighting profession's name for what we call a light bulb or tube.

local area network (LAN):
A group of computers connected so that they may share resources like peripheral devices and, possibly, access to other computers.

lumen:
Unit of light output.

luminaire:
A lighting fixture.

matte:
The opposite of shiny; a dull finish that doesn't reflect much light.

megabyte (MB):
A unit of memory measure equal to 1,024 kilobytes or 1,048,576 bytes.

memory:
Computer component that acts like a filing cabinet providing storage room for information.

microprocessor:
The "brain" of the computer, an integrated circuit or chip on the computer's main circuit board that processes instructions supplied to it by software.

motion sensor:
Device that turns the lights off whenever people are not around.

National Electrical Code:
The most widely accepted listing of minimum standards for electrical installations in the United States.

NIOSH:
National Institute of Occupational Safety and Health.

Noise Reduction Coefficient (NRC):
Standard measurement for the absorption of sound.

nomadic management:
Method of supervising all aspects of a business by wandering from department to department to stay in close contact with employees and their projects.

nonterritorial office:
Office layout in which common territories replace or substitute for desks traditionally "owned" by individuals.

open office:
Typically, this layout places the manager's desk in the foreground, within view of all other desks and enclosed spaces. The first open office appeared around 1960, when it was introduced in Germany as the "office landscape."

outlet:
A set of openings containing electrical contacts into which an electrical device can be plugged.

panel system:
Workstation defined by thin panels that provide privacy and insulation from noise.

parallel processing:
Using more than one central processing unit (CPU) to process parts of a problem concurrently.

particleboard:
A structural product made by bonding wood particles with synthetic resins under heat and pressure. Sometimes used in both building and furniture construction.

peripheral device:
A piece of computer hardware—such as a disk drive or printer—used in conjunction with a computer and under the computer's control. Such devices are usually separate from the computer and connected to it by wires or cables.

plenum:
The space between the ceiling tiles and the structural ceiling of an office that typically houses HVAC ducts, cabling for data and telecommunications, and electrical wiring.

random-access memory (RAM):
The part of the computer memory that stores information temporarily while you're working on it.

read-only memory (ROM):
The part of memory that contains information the computer uses (along with system files) throughout the system, including the information it needs to get itself started.

receptacle:
An electrical accessory that contains one (simplex) or two (duplex) outlets.

senior spike:
The large portion of the baby boom generation that is approaching 50.

sick building syndrome (SBS):
Phenomenon of employee discomfort and illness, or

perceived illness, due mainly to a polluted indoor air supply. An office is diagnosed "sick" when more than 20% of its occupants exhibit typical symptoms, complaints persists for two weeks or more and disappear when sufferers are away from the building.

smart building:
Also commonly referred to as the "intelligent" building. A centrally managed structure that offers advanced technology and shared tenant services.

software:
Instructions for the computer to carry out. The computer reads these instructions from disks inserted into the disk drive or from a hard disk.

sound masking:
Background sound that helps prevent office workers from being distracted by specific noises.

sound transmission class (STC):
standard measurement for the blocking of sound.

systems furniture:
Pieces of office furniture that can be combined and integrated in a variety of ways depending on the needs of the business.

task lighting:
Lighting that illuminates a specific task area or work surface.

timesharing computers:
Powerful systems that enable a large number of people to carry on simultaneous interactions through terminals that may be located a great distance from the central computer and its store of data.

veiling reflection:
Reflection from a bright light source such as a window or light fixture that is superimposed on an object. This partially or totally obscures details because the contrast is reduced.

VDT:
Video display terminal. Often used to refer to a mainframe terminal.

volt:
The force that produces current flow in an electrical circuit.

voltage spike:
An extremely high voltage increase on an electrical circuit that lasts only a fraction of a second, but can damage sensitive electronic equipment.

war room:
Also called a "solutions room." This is an enclosed area with a large table that is used for decision-making or strategy-making meetings.

watt:
A unit of electrical consumption. When the power requirement of a device is listed in watts, you can convert to amps by dividing the wattage by the voltage (e.g., 1,200 watts, divided by 120 volts, equal 10 amps).

workstation:
Furniture manufacturers use this term to define all the furniture and accessories contained in the space occupied by an office worker. Computer makers use it to define a powerful computer for an individual user, usually networked to other workstations or to a mainframe computer.

CREDITS

Concept
Richard Wurman

Editorial
Maura Carey Damacion
additional writing:
Rebecca Ellis
Richard Wurman
Lisa Zuniga

Design
Michael Everitt
Nathan Shedroff

Illustrations
Charles Shields
additional illustrations:
Sherrod Blankner

Photos
Art Center College of
Design
Image Bank
Steelcase Inc.
Super Stock

Printing and Binding
Webcom Limited
Mike Collinge
Ciri DeLuca

Special Thanks
Paul Allie
Autodesk, Inc.
Babey Moulton, Inc.
Steve Brown
Building Owners and
Managers Association
International
Niels Diffrient
Steve Eldersveld
Gerard Garbutt
Gensler and Associates
Architects
Kevin Gilfillan
Grid Systems Corporation
Chuck Halterman
Randy Helm
Pacific Bell
Salk Institute
Roger Sliker
Howard Sutton
United Airlines
Don Wheeler
Xerox Palo Alto Research
Center

Steelcase ®

As The Office Environment Company serving companies worldwide, Steelcase has sponsored this book to help people understand the elements essential to a healthy, safe, comfortable, and productive office. **OFFICE ACCESS** serves as a guide to current office issues. It contains a broad range of practical information in an easily accessible format. We believe **OFFICE ACCESS** will help virtually everyone working in an office including entrepreneurs establishing new businesses, individuals interested in maximizing their environment to meet specific needs, and professionals who help shape effective office environments. We hope you find it enjoyable as well as helpful.

TUB

The**Understanding**Business is an Information Design and Electronic Publishing firm in San Francisco. TUB has created extraordinary guides to medicine, baseball, the Olympics and even the *Wall Street Journal*. The Understanding Business has also designed and produced the **ACCESS**® travel guides for US and worldwide destinations and created the Pacific Bell **SMART** YellowPages in California. TUB solves communication problems and creates unique design products that make complex information clear, memorable and useful.

President/Creative Director
Mark Johnson

Design Director
Mark Goldman

Principal Designer
Stuart Silberman

Senior Designer
Tom Beatty

Project Manager
Megan Foley

The**Understanding**Business
1160 Battery Street
San Francisco, CA 94111
TEL   415 616 4800
FAX   415 616 4899

Technical notes...
OFFICE ACCESS was designed and produced using Apple Macintosh™ computers. Layout was done in PageMaker 4.2™ while all illustrations were produced with Adobe Illustrator 3.0™. Film was generated directly from disk using a Hyphen RIP output to Crosfield Flatbed Imagesetters. Otabind™, a unique lay-flat binding process, was used to insure user friendliness and durability. **Printed in Canada.**
S-298